# Transformational Change in Higher Education

# Transformational Change in Higher Education

Positioning Colleges and Universities for Future Success

*Edited by*

Madeleine B. d'Ambrosio
*TIAA-CREF Institute, USA*

Ronald G. Ehrenberg
*Cornell University, USA*

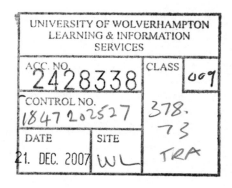
IN ASSOCIATION WITH TIAA-CREF

**Edward Elgar**
Cheltenham, UK • Northampton, MA, USA

Published by
Edward Elgar Publishing Limited
Glensanda House
Montpellier Parade
Cheltenham
Glos GL50 1UA
UK

Edward Elgar Publishing, Inc.
William Pratt House
9 Dewey Court
Northampton
Massachusetts 01060
USA

A catalogue record for this book
is available from the British Library

**Library of Congress Cataloging-in-Publication Data**

d'Ambrosio, Madeleine, 1950–
    Transformational change in higher education : positioning colleges and universities for future success / Madeleine B. d'Ambrosio, Ronald G. Ehrenberg.
        p.   cm.
    Includes bibliographical references and index.
    1. Education, Higher—Aims and objectives—United States. 2. Education, Higher—United States—Administration. 3. Universities and colleges—United States—Planning. 4. Educational change—United States. I. Ehrenberg, Ronald G.   II. TIAA-CREF Institute. III. Title.

LA227.4.D346   2007
378.73—dc22
                                                                                            2007039424
ISBN 978 1 84720 252 9

Printed and bound in Great Britain by MPG Books Ltd, Bodmin, Cornwall

# Contents

# Contributors

## AUTHORS

**F. King Alexander** President, California State University, Long Beach and University of Wisconsin System

**Herbert M. Allison Jr** Chairman, President and Chief Executive Officer, TIAA-CREF

**Patrick M. Callan** President, National Center for Public Policy and Higher Education

**Madeleine B. d'Ambrosio** Vice President and Executive Director, TIAA-CREF Institute

**Ronald G. Ehrenberg** Irving M. Ives Professor of Industrial and Labor Relations and Economics, Cornell University; Director of the Cornell Higher Education Research Institute; TIAA-CREF Institute Fellow

**James C. Hearn** Professor, Institute of Higher Education, University of Georgia; TIAA-CREF Institute Fellow

**Donald E. Heller** Director, Center for the Study of Higher Education, and Associate Professor of Education, Pennsylvania State University; TIAA-CREF Institute Fellow

**Robert M. O'Neil** Professor of Law, University Professor, and Director of the Thomas Jefferson Center for the Protection of Free Expression, University of Virginia; former President of the University of Virginia

# PANELISTS AND MODERATORS

**Walé Adeosun** Treasurer and Chief Investment Officer, Rensselaer Polytechnic Institute

**F. King Alexander** (see list of authors)

**Lawrence S. Bacow** President, Tufts University

**Gerald L. Baliles** Former Governor of Virginia and Director of the Miller Center for Public Affairs at the University of Virginia

**Carol A. Cartwright** President Emeritus, Kent State University

**Scott S. Cowen** President, Tulane University

**Ronald G. Ehrenberg** (see list of authors)

**Dolores M. Fernández** President, Hostos Community College, City University of New York

**Alan Finder** Education reporter, *The New York Times*

**Roy Flores** Chancellor, Pima Community College

**Mildred García** President, Berkeley College of New York and New Jersey

**James C. Garland** President Emeritus, Miami University of Ohio

**Gordon Gee** President, Ohio State University

**Catharine Bond Hill** President, Vassar College

**Scott Kaspick** Managing Director, Kaspick and Company

**William E. Kirwan** Chancellor, University System of Maryland

**Richard D. Legon** President, Association of Governing Boards of Universities and Colleges (AGB)

**James T. McGill** Senior Vice President, Finance and Administration, Johns Hopkins University

**Harold W. Pote** Trustee, Drexel University; President and CEO, American Financial Realty Trust

**James Scannell** President, Scannell & Kurz, Inc.

**Alvin J. Schexnider** President, Schexnider & Associates, LLC; former Executive Vice President, Norfolk State University

**David J. Skorton** President, Cornell University

**Robert G. Templin Jr** President, Northern Virginia Community College

**Laura Skandera Trombley** President, Pitzer College

**David Ward** President, American Council on Education (ACE)

# Foreword

## Herbert M. Allison Jr

In the face of ever increasing pressures within the business of higher education, transformational change has become a prevalent theme for academic leaders. Forces necessitating change are many, including daunting fiscal and demographic challenges; increasing demands regarding access, affordability and accountability; the rapid pace of technological advances; increased competition among institutions for both students and faculty; and demands to upgrade and expand facilities. Such forces will continue to stretch budgets that are already constrained and challenge traditional ways of operating. The best leaders will see this as an era of opportunity for American colleges and universities and will adapt their paradigms and their models to embrace and foster evolving teaching roles, learning preferences, and research and outreach missions.

At TIAA-CREF, we are building on our historic mission of partnering with higher education, our core market, to help address challenges such as those described above, to meet institutions' needs and those of their employees. Acting as a bridge between higher education and our company, the TIAA-CREF Institute generates research, information and understanding focused on financial security and higher education issues. The Institute shares this knowledge through its books, periodicals, DVDs, conferences, webcasts and other forums. This volume, part of the TIAA-CREF Institute Series on Higher Education, is one example of our commitment to providing new and actionable information to higher education leadership to enhance decision making and inform strategic planning.

In November 2006, the Institute convened Transformational Change in Higher Education: Positioning Your Institution for Future Success, a major national conference of university presidents, chancellors, academic deans, scholars and others to examine how their institutions can successfully adapt to the rapidly changing higher education landscape.

Conference attendees first considered how successful leaders can align their institutional vision and initiatives with the expectations of the diverse groups of stakeholders they serve (governing boards, policymakers and the public) and achieve an environment conducive to transformational change. The conference next provided a forum for academic leaders to exchange ideas on issues of strategic importance, such as increasing student access through strategic pricing initiatives and developing creative financing strategies for higher education. We are indebted to our conference participants who brought their experiences to the table and shared their unique perspectives.

This book includes chapters devoted to each of the thematic issues covered by the conference. The input of the more than 100 higher education thought leaders who attended the conference is also reflected throughout these pages. The chapters were written by a distinguished group of prominent higher education scholars, who not only summarized and synthesized the presentations and discussions of each conference session but also shared their personal thinking and insights regarding the issues raised. We are very grateful for their efforts.

TIAA-CREF is proud to once again explore issues of strategic importance to higher education with those we serve through the TIAA-CREF Institute's National Higher Education Leadership Conferences. We at TIAA-CREF are privileged to serve our partners in higher education, and look forward to continuing our longstanding collaboration with them.

# Introduction

## Ronald G. Ehrenberg and Madeleine B. d'Ambrosio

## CHANGING ISSUES, ENVIRONMENT AND EXPECTATIONS

Higher education institutional leaders and higher education policy-makers in the United States face daunting challenges in the years ahead. Inequities in college-going rates across students from different socioeconomic and racial/ethnic groups have narrowed only slightly during the past 30 years and inequities in college completion rates have narrowed even less. The fastest growing groups in the United States are those that have been historically underrepresented in higher education and, as our economy becomes increasingly knowledge based, higher education becomes more essential both for these individuals' economic well-being and for our nation's productivity growth.

Tuition at our nation's private colleges and universities increased during the period at rates that exceeded the rate of inflation by about 3 percent a year and tuition as a share of family income has grown substantially. Posted tuition levels overstate the cost of college to students because the typical private college or university recycles almost 40 percent of its tuition revenues back to students in the form of grant aid. However, increasingly private colleges and universities award institutional grant aid based on 'merit' rather than need, as they seek to use their financial aid policies to help 'craft' their entering class, rather than to guarantee access. The major growth of federal financial support has been in the form of subsidized loans and tax credits, which benefit primarily students from middle-income families, rather than in the form of grant aid for students from lower-income families. Following the development of the Georgia Hope Scholarship programs, state financial aid programs for students have also been increasingly merit rather than need based.

Approximately two-thirds of American four-year college students and four-fifths of all American college students are educated at public higher education institutions. Over the last 30 years enrollment at these institutions has more than doubled. In real terms, state appropriations per full-time equivalent student at these institutions have remained roughly flat over the period, as states have faced both tax-payers' desires to cut, or limit, the growth of state taxes and increasing demands on resources from elementary and secondary education, Medicaid, and the criminal justice system. Put simply, public higher education is one of the few discretionary items in state budgets and financial pressures make it likely that states will not be able to substantially increase their real level of appropriations to public higher education in the future.

As a result, in an effort to maintain their quality and keep up with their private competitors, public universities have increased their tuition at rates equal to or exceeding private higher education. However, because their tuitions started out so much lower, the absolute dollar increases that they received from these increases were much smaller than those their private counterparts received from their tuition increases, and expenditures per student at the publics have fallen relative to expenditures per student at their private counterparts. Not surprisingly, faculty salaries in public education have fallen relative to faculty salaries in private higher education, which makes it increasingly difficult for the publics to attract and retain top faculty, and the publics (and to a lesser extent the privates) have increasingly substituted part-time and full-time non-tenure-track faculty for full-time tenure-track faculty in an effort to hold down their costs. However, there is no such thing as a 'free lunch' and careful research shows that lower expenditures per student and an increased use of 'contingent faculty' are both associated with lower graduation rates.

A substantial fraction of America's full-time college faculty members are approaching retirement ages; estimates are that as many as one-third of faculty members will be retiring in the next 10–15 years. These retirements, plus the increasing number of faculty that will be required to help meet projected increases in enrollments, provide an almost unprecedented opportunity for America's colleges and universities to diversify their faculty along racial, ethnic and gender lines. However, the fraction of American college students going on for PhDs is much lower now than it was years ago and institutions legitimately worry about whether they will be able to find the next generation of faculty members. The competition for new faculty is likely to bid up faculty salaries, increasing the financial problems that universities face, and increasing the tendency to search for cheaper ways to deliver higher education.

The public and private non-profit higher education sectors are also being buffeted by a growing for-profit higher education sector. Represented by well-known institutions such as the University of Phoenix and Devry, this sector puts additional pressures on public and private academic institutions to hold down their costs and to more efficiently deliver education. Institutions increasingly are exploring how technology can increase the efficiency of their education operations; a number of institutions now require students to take a specified number of classes online to relieve capacity constraints facing on-campus learning. More generally, institutions are examining whether technological innovation can enhance the amount of learning that goes on at college campuses, even if it does not reduce costs.

While it often appears that the parents are preoccupied with college costs, they are also passionately concerned with the perceived quality of the college experience. The competition for students is fierce and the expectations of students and parents for what college should provide keep increasing. Traditional double rooms in dormitories, gyms, and dining halls are replaced by residential living centers with students living in suites, fitness centers (and climbing walls) and dining facilities in which omelets can be cooked to order. Tiered classrooms become a must, as do coffee shops in the library, and completely wired campuses for easy internet access. Balancing the demand for such facilities with efforts to moderate tuition increases cost is no easy task for administrators.

Higher education is also being buffeted by increasing expectations that the research its faculty members do will lead to improvements in the population's well-being and will serve as a vehicle for economic development. To justify their state support, public higher education institutions increasingly seek to document their contributions to the state above and beyond the students that they educate. And, more generally, higher education is facing the pressures to be more accountable for both the public support that it receives and the payments from parents and students.

These forces are all leading to the need for higher education institutions to transform themselves and adapt to the changing environment in which they operate and the changing demands that are being placed on them. It was natural then for the TIAA-CREF Institute's November 2006 National Higher Education Leadership Conference, Transformational Change in Higher Education: Positioning Your Institution for Future Success, to be directed at these issues.

The Institute's previous National Higher Education Leadership Conferences each consisted primarily of presentations and discussions of commissioned papers and each led to a published volume.[1] To expand the range of participants, this conference and thus this volume were structured differently. A series of roundtable discussions were held, with each followed by audience participation and questions. Transcripts of these sessions were then provided to a set of distinguished higher education researchers and policymakers and each was asked to provide us with a paper that summarized the discussion at a session and his own 'take' on the issues that the session raised. Participants were given an opportunity to comment on the authors' drafts to ensure they were not misquoted and the authors revised their papers taking this feedback into account.

*Transformational Change in Higher Education* is the result of this process and we briefly summarize below the subject matter discussed in each of the five chapters that follow. At the conclusion of the first day of the conference, Herbert M. Allison Jr, Chairman, President and Chief Executive Officer of TIAA-CREF, gave a presentation on the transformational change that TIAA-CREF itself had made following the 1997 federal government decision to begin taxing the income it produced. Many conference participants felt that his presentation, which detailed the efforts by TIAA-CREF to become responsive to its customers needs and to rethink its whole business plan and methods of operation, contained lessons that were important for college and university leaders to hear. Consequently, we prevailed upon him to transform his remarks into the paper which became the concluding chapter of this volume.

## SETTING THE STAGE

The first session was moderated by Alan Finder, an education reporter for the *New York Times*. This session sought to provide a context for the remainder of the conference by addressing features of the current higher education landscape that are prompting transformational change which relate to interactions with key constituencies, how higher education is financed, and issues of student access. The session participants included two leaders of major private research universities, each of whom has also been a leader of a public research university, Gordon Gee (Chancellor of Vanderbilt University)[2] and David Skorton (President of Cornell University); a leader of a public comprehensive university, F. King Alexander (President of California State University, Long Beach); and a community college leader, Dolores M. Fernández (President of Hostos Community College of the City University of New York). King Alexander, who is also a noted researcher in the area of educational finance, wrote the chapter summarizing the session.

This chapter discusses how rising societal expectations coincide with important fiscal realities from the perspective of college and university presidents from each of the primary postsecondary sectors. The presidents discussed an array of challenges, strategies and issues that will continue to place internal and external pressures on institutional leaders throughout the nation. Unfortunately, positioning their colleges and universities for future success in an increasingly competitive academic marketplace that is destined to continue to place significant premiums on top students, high quality faculty, and expensive educational opportunities is not their only challenge.

Societal pressure to provide greater access, improve student completion rates, limit expenditures, control tuition more judiciously, and fuel the economy with new ideas and innovative human capital are all issues that have become critical factors in assessing college and university productivity. At the heart of these multiple challenges for postsecondary education leaders resides the ongoing struggle to balance building institutional stability through enhancing educational quality, maximizing national prestige, and securing financial wealth with the more egalitarian needs of a society that does not fully comprehend the fiscal ramifications of their expectations.

Many of the issues addressed by these presidents in this chapter are among the most controversial and perplexing to the public at large and include increasing institutional expenditures, rising student tuition and fees, enhancing accountability, and measuring quality. The presidents also delved into the pressures associated with private fund raising, athletics, and other individual issues that impact important

decisions and strategies that add to the complexity of modern collegiate leadership.

## STRENGTHENING THE ACADEMIC PRESIDENCY

American higher education is governed through a system of shared
governance between faculty, administrators and trustees. The saying
'trying to lead the faculty is like trying to herd cats' has often been
used to describe one of the challenges that university presidents face.
Another is building relationships with an institution's board of
trustees, and more specifically with the chair of the board, which
facilitate the president's leadership and allow the shared vision of the
board and the president for the development of the institution to be
developed.[3]

Given the key roles of presidents and trustees, the second session
dealt with efforts to strengthen the leadership capacity of presidents
and recommendations for improving the relationship between
trustees and presidents that came from a recent Association of
Governing Boards (AGB) Task Force on the State of the Presidency
in American Higher Education. The panel was moderated by Richard
D. Legon, President of the Association of Governing Boards, and
included Gerald L. Baliles, former governor of Virginia (who in this
role appointed numerous trustees to the boards of public colleges and
universities in Virginia and who also chaired the AGB task force);
Harold W. Pote, a trustee of Drexel University; Alvin Schexnider,
Executive Vice President of Norfolk State University; and Laura
Skandera Trombley, President of Pitzer College. Robert O'Neil, a
former President of the University of Virginia and the University of
Wisconsin statewide system and currently Professor of Law and
Director of the Thomas Jefferson Center for the Protection of Free
Expression at the University of Virginia, authored the paper sum-
marizing the session.

The themes in this session were numerous but a few stood out. One
was the importance of making the relationship between the governing board and the president a collaborative one. A second was for
board members to have an understanding of the truly stressful nature
of the presidency and of the importance of their providing continual
support for the president. This will be easier for the board to do if

their search process ensures that the president not only displays leadership and management skills but also has a true passion for higher education and their institution. A third is the importance of the board facilitating the transition of a new leader into the presidency. A fourth is the role of the chair of the board in supporting the president's personal health and welfare.

The session also stressed the equal importance of the choice of a board chair and the choice of a president, the importance of evaluation and assessment of the performance of both the president and the board, the importance of strategic planning, and the importance of carefully managing the transition at the end of a president's term as well as the transition into the presidency. Finally, a major theme was the complex roles and responsibilities of the trustees themselves, how these roles were rapidly changing because of the public demand for greater transparency, and how both the selection and retention (or lack of retention) processes for trustees can have a major impact on the well-being of an institution.

# ALIGNING INSTITUTIONAL VISIONS WITH POLICYMAKERS' AND THE PUBLIC'S INTERESTS

The success of a higher education institution, including its prospects for financial support from external constituents, depends heavily on its ability to create an alignment between its strategic vision for its role in society and the views of the public and government officials regarding the mission of higher education. The third session of the conference explored how leaders build understanding and how growing public pressure for accountability impacts the development and communication of a strategic vision. This session was moderated by David Ward, President of the American Council on Education (and former Chancellor of the University of Wisconsin-Madison) and its participants included three presidents of private institutions – Lawrence S. Bacow (Tufts University), Scott S. Cowen (Tulane University) and Mildred García (Berkeley College) – and William E. Kirwan, the Chancellor of the University System of Maryland. Patrick Callan, President of the National Center for Public Policy and Higher Education, wrote the paper summarizing this session.

While the discussion at this session reflected the institutional perspectives of the different presenters, a number of important themes emerged. First, transformational change is difficult because of the difficulty of aligning the interests of all of the participants. The public are much more concerned about costs than they are about accountability; however, they are also concerned about the quality of what is being provided and, unlike in the business world, competition in higher education often leads to increased amenities and higher costs, not reduced costs.

Second, what institutions see as being in their best interest may not always be in the social interest. For example, the substantial growth in the use of merit aid to help craft 'desirable classes' and improve institutions' *U.S. News & World Report* rankings (discussed above), which has redirected financial aid resources away from students from lower-income families to those from middle- and upper-income families, has hindered efforts to improve access in the United States. Or, to take another example, the preoccupation of higher education leaders and policymakers with higher education's role in improving global competitiveness may cause institutions to lose sight of the traditional mission of liberal education.

Third, transformational change is difficult, but 'enlightened incrementalism' leading to improvements in higher education is much more feasible and occurs on an ongoing basis in higher education. While enlightened incrementalism occurs as a result of institutions' desires to be more effective than they have been in the past, transformational change can occur only as a result of major crises that threaten the survival of an institution and the area in which it is located. Scott Cowen's discussion of how Tulane responded to the crisis caused by Hurricane Katrina emphasized this point; the restructuring of Tulane that occurred, which he believes has substantially improved the institution, could not have taken place without the pressures caused by the crisis.

Fourth, higher education institutions, including the proprietary ones (represented on the panel by Berkeley College), should recognize that state and federal governments have a legitimate interest in their quality, costs and administration. Rather than seeking to avoid accountability, institutions should embrace the concept and work with policymakers to develop meaningful regulatory procedures. Similarly, to justify increases in state funding, public universities should take steps to demonstrate (as the University System of Maryland did) that they are responsive to public needs and taking actions to improve their efficiency.

In his concluding comments, Pat Callan notes three major examples of transformational change that have taken place in higher education: the Land Grant Acts, which led to the establishment of state colleges and universities; the GI Bill and federal funding of research after World War II, which led to rapid expansion of higher education and the development of research universities; and the growth in community colleges in response to the baby boomer generation. He suggests that each of these involved institutional responses to a major social change and that these responses required new missions, policies or structures.

Callan believes that potential transformational change in American higher education in the decade ahead will be driven by a set of forces that include the emergence of a knowledge based global economy, the need to replace baby boomers in the work force by students who are coming from lower income families and ethnic communities that have been traditionally underrepresented in American higher education, by financial constraints faced by federal and state governments, by rapidly increasing education levels in many of our economic competitors, by the possibilities of the growing use of technology in higher education, by public pressure to increase college completion rates and to measure learning outcomes and by the growing sense that there is a national interest in higher education. How higher education responds to these forces will go a long way towards determining our nation's future.

## FINANCING INSTITUTIONAL OPERATIONS: THE ENTREPRENEURIAL LEADER

Given tuition increases that have long exceeded the rates of inflation and the declining ability of states to finance their public higher education institutions with state appropriations, higher education leaders have long understood that they need to diversify their revenue streams, seek alternative sources of revenue, and try to reduce their cost structure. The fourth session addressed the strategies that institutions are pursuing to diversify revenue sources, to finance their capital expenditures, and to reduce their costs.

The session was moderated by Scott Kaspick, President of Kaspick and Company (the nation's leading provider of planned-giving services for colleges, universities and other non-profits. Kaspick was acquired by TIAA-CREF in 2006). Its participants included Roy Flores, the Chancellor of Pima Community College; Walé Adeosun, the Treasurer and Chief Investment Officer at Rensselaer Polytechnic Institute; James McGill, the Senior Vice President for Finance and Administration at Johns Hopkins University; and Carol Cartwright, President Emeritus of Kent State University. James Hearn, a higher education finance researcher from the University of Georgia, authored the essay that summarized the session.

Each participant highlighted some of the steps that his or her institution had recently undertaken. Under the leadership of its president, Shirley Ann Jackson, Rensselaer worked hard to improve its enrollment management (increasing its applicant pool, improving retention and reducing tuition discounting), to diversify and expand its flow of research funding, to improve its annual fund raising and its endowment investment strategies, and to develop strategic partnerships with corporations to meet capital needs.

Echoing Scott Cowen's discussion in the previous session, Carol Cartwright discussed the importance of a leader's standing up and defining reality to faculty and staff to get them to buy into the need for change when faced with a financial crisis. She empowered key administrators to become part of the solution and fulfilled Kent State's need to develop substantial funding to upgrade and expand its residence halls by working with Lehman Brothers to develop a creative way to achieve large debt financing at a relatively low guaranteed cost. The university's administration allocated resources to new programs that could demonstrate their ability to increase overall enrollment (and thus tuition revenues), worked at ways to reduce the costs of existing programs (without reducing their quality) and instituted some 'premium' tuition and fee charges for expensive programs that promised great financial rewards to students. Finally, they sought legislative changes that would allow them to improve their financial position (such as more freedom as to how to invest working capital and endowments) and aggressively sought ways to commercialize their faculty members' research findings. They did not, however, engage in widespread outsourcing, because they wanted to maintain control over the quality of their operations.

Roy Flores stressed the importance of providing financial training for all administrators at his college and then providing them with incentives to only create programs that promise to break even within three years or that meet an important social need. The college also has created partnerships with the University of Arizona both to provide revenue for the college (delivering remedial education to UA students who require it) and to ensure the smooth transition of Pima graduates to the UA. Finally, it has created partnerships with a variety of local employers to help meet their needs for trained individuals to staff specific occupations (for example, nurses and engineers); in doing so it has generated revenue for the institution and also helped to meet important social needs.

After presenting a general discussion of the financial issues facing research universities, James McGill proposed a number of strategies that they could pursue to improve their cost structures. These included investing more in administrative technologies, developing new models for research management and, counter to the view expressed by Cartwright, exploring outsourcing of administrative applications. Put simply, he argued that research universities should focus much more heavily on cost reduction; this would reduce the need to develop new revenue streams.

In his summary of the issues raised by, and not considered by, the session, James Hearn placed the discussion in the broader context of the issues higher education is facing. He cautioned that some social objectives, for example increasing retention and graduation rates, will require more resources, not less. Successful financial innovation on campuses must be tied to underlying academic values.

## CHANGING STUDENT ACCESS THROUGH STRATEGIC PRICING INITIATIVES

The fifth session was moderated by Ronald Ehrenberg and the participants were James Garland, President Emeritus of Miami University (Ohio); James Scannell, President of Scannell & Kurz, Inc.; Catharine Bond Hill, President of Vassar College; and Robert G. Templin Jr, President of Northern Virginia Community College. Donald Heller from Pennsylvania State University wrote the paper summarizing the session. The session dealt with how strategic pricing has emerged as a tool in managing the recruitment and retention of students and the changes in other institutional policies that have emerged.

Building on the innovative tuition policy that he developed while he was President of Miami University, Garland proposed moving to

a system of financing of public higher education in which state appropriations to public higher education institutions for undergraduate
education would be eliminated and the dollar value of these appropriations transferred to students in the form of vouchers that could
be used at any public or private higher education institution in the
state. Public higher education institutions would have to charge
market tuition levels and to compete with private higher education
institutions in the state for students. The vouchers would go only to
the subset of students with financial need; the system would thus both
promote access and lead to increased efficiencies.

Catharine Bond Hill discussed the implications of research that she
and her former colleague, Gordon Winston of Williams, conducted
on enrollment outcomes for students from different socioeconomic
backgrounds at a set of selective private colleges and universities.
Although these institutions admit students without consideration of
their financial need and provide need-based financial aid that is
sufficient to make them viable alternatives for talented students from
lower-income families, in fact very few students from lower-income
families were admitted to and enrolled at these institutions. Their subsequent research suggested that there were a much larger number of
talented students from lower-income families who could meet the
admission standards at these institutions and Hill speculated about
the forces that continue to cause these students to be underrepresented at selective private colleges and universities. Hill and Winston's
research is very important and the publicity that it received was at
least partially responsible for the development of a number of programs that the richest selective private colleges and universities have
instituted to try to enhance their enrollment of talented students from
lower-income families.

James Scannell, who previously served in high-level enrollment
management leadership positions at Cornell University and the
University or Rochester, talked about how the strategic use of institutional financial aid at less selective public and private institutions
can both improve the academic profile of an entering class and
increase the number of students that institutions can afford to enroll
from lower-income families. He stressed the use of empirical models
of students' enrollment decisions in developing institutional financial
aid policies.

The final participant, Robert Templin, discussed an innovative
policy that the state of Virginia was contemplating pursuing to

encourage the education of its growing immigrant population, many of whom are coming from relatively low-income families in which tuition is likely to be a barrier to higher education enrollment and persistence. The state is creating a Community College Transfer Scholarship, in which students who graduate from Virginia community colleges with at least a B average, come from families with incomes of less than 150 percent of the state median, and are admitted and transfer to a public college or university in the state would be able to attend that institution for up to 70 credit hours during a three-year period and continue to pay the lower community college tuition rates. The state hopes that this will encourage more students with college aspirations to start at community colleges (thereby saving the state money) and to enhance their college completion rates. The flagship publics in the state would benefit because this would enhance their ability to expand their enrollment of students from lower-income families (state subsidies would make up for some or all of their lost tuition revenue from the lower tuition that these transfer students would be paying).

Don Heller's essay places these strategies in the context of more general federal, state and institutional policies that relate to student access. He stresses that improving access and persistence is one of the key challenges that higher education faces and that the specific policies that these essays address are but a few of the different policy responses that will need to be developed in the years ahead.

# LESSONS FOR ACADEMIA FROM TIAA-CREF'S RESTRUCTURING

The final chapter of this volume is a revision of the address that Herbert Allison gave at the conference on how TIAA-CREF transformed itself when confronted by a major change in 1997, the loss of its tax exempt status. The transformation process, which he led after being appointed CEO, clarified in his own mind the principles that can help leaders of organizations of any kind to effectively respond to changes in the environment that they face and ensure the continuing success of their institutions. As we noted earlier, conference participants judged his remarks to be so useful that we have included the revised address here so that it will be widely disseminated to the higher education community.

Allison's essay deals with how a leader of an institution that has a long-term record of success and has become complacent (a description appropriate perhaps for many higher education institutions) can cause the institution to embrace necessary change when facing a rapidly changing environment and a growing number of competitors. If the institution is to be successful, it will need to make fundamental decisions about its priorities and will require previously unthinkable transformation of its programs and infrastructure.

Allison stresses that no leader can compel an organization to make fundamental change by logical arguments or force of authority. Rather, echoing remarks made in several earlier chapters, he says it is essential that all participants in the organization are enabled to see for themselves that change is imperative. He did this when he arrived at TIAA-CREF in late 2002 by asking 60 respected TIAA-CREF middle managers to form teams to study the organization's market position, its customers' needs, its technological capabilities, its human resource policies and programs, its financial situation and its investment performance, and then to recommend strategies going forward. Within six months they reported back with radical recommended changes and a plan to bring colleagues on board and to successfully lead the change.

By making changes in an open and transparent way and directing savings towards the core missions of the institution, Allison built strong support from the very people whose organizational units would have to change. So a key message for higher education is to encourage stakeholders at many levels – students, faculty, staff, administrators, unions, policymakers and trustees – all to gather the facts and come to grips with them. Only by encouraging people to deal with the issues themselves can a leader generate real buy-in and ownership of systematic changes.

Once an institution begins on the process of transformational change, how can a leader institutionalize the process of change so that the institution will continue to prosper in the future? Here Allison argues that the institution must define its long-term mission broadly and design the organization to be always alert to new methods to meet its fundamental mission. Put simply, instilling a sense of the importance of the mission, not of the current institutional form, is essential if an organization is to keep moving forward.

TIAA-CREF is dedicated to serving the needs of the academic community. In discussing how the organization transformed itself and the principles by which this transformation took, and is continuing to take, place, Allison's essay should help serve the need of academia to engage in thinking about transformational change.

## NOTES

1. The two previous volumes in the TIAA-CREF Institute Series on Higher Education that resulted from these conferences are Robert Clark and Madeleine d'Ambrosio (eds), *The New Balancing Act in the Business of Higher Education* (Cheltenham, UK and Northampton, MA, USA: Edward Elgar, 2006), and Robert Clark and Jennifer Ma (eds), *Recruitment, Retention and Retirement in Higher Education: Building and Managing the Faculty of the Future* (Cheltenham, UK and Northampton, MA, USA: Edward Elgar, 2005).
2. Subsequent to the conference, Gee became the President of Ohio State University for the second time.
3. James O. Freedman, former President of both the University of Iowa and Dartmouth College, describes the differences in the roles that the boards of private and public institutions play and the interaction of an academic institution's president with each in 'Presidents and trustees' in Ronald G. Ehrenberg (ed.), *Governing Academia* (Ithaca, NY: Cornell University Press, 2005).

# 1. Balancing the challenges of today with the promise of tomorrow: a presidential perspective

**F. King Alexander**

During the last decade many profound challenges have emerged for colleges and universities throughout much of the world. These challenges have significantly reshaped the higher education landscape and forced institutional leaders to face important fiscal, managerial and educational pressures. Most of these pressures have been generated by the success of the higher education enterprise and the societal expectations that have followed. In this chapter I will highlight some of the more important issues and concerns impacting colleges and universities today according to four American college and university presidents who were invited to discuss these challenges as part of a presidential panel moderated by *New York Times* higher education columnist Alan Finder. The event was undertaken as an open exchange of ideas and focused on a wide variety of current trends and public issues. Participating in this discussion were President Gordon Gee from Vanderbilt University, who brought over 27 years of university leadership experience to the panel; President David Skorton from Cornell University and the former President of the University of Iowa; President Dolores Fernández from Hostos Community College in New York; and myself. What ultimately emerged from the panel's dialogue and commentary were four principal macro themes or issues: the changing higher education landscape, college costs and prices, public accountability and scrutiny, and philanthropy. The panel discussants sought to describe how their respective colleges and universities are coping with these emergent issues while also exploring some of the strategies and ideas that are being implemented to stay ahead of the curve. The chapter will also delve into the reasons why many of these issues are likely to persist or assume differing emphases, placing further pressure on institutions and their leaders to reposition their campuses for the future.

## THE CHANGING HIGHER EDUCATION LANDSCAPE

Prior to addressing the specific challenges and issues permeating the higher education environment today, it is important to understand the complexity of the changing educational landscape and to recognize the expanding societal demands that are coalescing in unprecedented ways. Commentary from each of the presidents indicated that there is broad consensus regarding the nature of the evolving environment of higher education and the demands being placed on institutions. However, their comments indicated uncertainty as to the ultimate role that each institution plays as societal demands manifest themselves in pressures that affect existing strategies developed to promote the welfare of individual colleges and universities. It is this dilemma, the pursuit of institutional success versus the challenge of meeting increased societal demands, that has made it very difficult for many campus leaders to find the appropriate balance. This has become an increasingly significant issue for many of the nation's most successful and prestigious universities who, despite their unprecedented wealth, continue to only provide very selective educational opportunities to underrepresented student populations.

Evidence of this trend was recently featured in a report ranking the most exclusive public and private universities by their lower-income enrollments (Mortenson, 2007). The report listed the top 50 most restrictive universities describing them as 'gated communities' because of their lack of commitment to lower-income student enrollments during the last decade as they have become more selective and wealthier as measured by endowment support and per student expenditures. This disturbing trend also was briefly alluded to in a *New York Times* article that featured one university's attempt to rethink their institutional strategy by expanding their entering classes regardless of the potential deleterious consequences in prestige that could result from such a decision (Applebome, 2007).

Despite the significance of this 'pursuit of prestige', the institutional leaders on this panel felt that this was an issue that only impacted a small number of public and private universities. For this small group of presidents there was a much more prominent and serious challenge currently facing higher education and that is providing universal post-secondary access to all students. In many ways we have become a product of our own success. Providing universal access to some form of postsecondary education for every student is a large-scale challenge which has emanated from the widespread success of higher education and the increasing recognition of human capital as a state or nation's most valued natural resource. This kind of urgent prioritization of the future value of human capital or educated talent has not always been the case in our nation or many nations throughout the world. For 50 years, while the world watched, the people of the United States debated whether every student should have an opportunity to attend some form of postsecondary education. The concept of 'universality' of access to higher education in the US was first advanced in 1945, and then in policy form by the Truman Commission in 1947. Unfortunately, the recommendations being advocated by the Commission met with fierce resistance, especially from many within the higher education community. Even the very successful Serviceman's Readjustment Act, also known as the GI Bill, which opened the door to education opportunities for American soldiers returning from World War II, was fiercely resisted by many. The University of Chicago's President Robert Maynard Hutchins and *New York Times* columnist Seymour Harris expressed the fear that opening of collegiate doors to returning soldiers was bad public policy and would turn our colleges and universities into 'hobo jungles'. For the next fifty years the recommendations of the Truman Commission calling for the 'universality' of higher education would become one of the most hotly contested public policy issues of the era. It was not until the late 1980s and early 1990s that the remaining political resistance to the concept of universal access to postsecondary education began to quietly fade from public discourse.

In the 1960s and 1970s, the last true period where substantial national dialogue occurred involving the role of the federal government in higher education, important public policies were developed where widespread access to higher education was advanced as a major policy theme despite resistance to the universal idea that still existed both within and in many areas outside academe. Within the higher education community during the 1970s and early 1980s, there persisted an attitude that not all persons should be students in higher education. This resulted in a common practice among many four-year institutions whereby students were readily eliminated from colleges and universities. This illustrated an inability of higher education to adapt and was one of the reasons why unprecedented dropout rates developed on many campuses nationwide during this period. Providing all students access was one thing, but adaptation to ensure that they could be retained and graduate proved increasingly difficult for many colleges and universities.

The national push for universal access to higher education also led to the massive expansion of the community college sector, which happened to be the first sector to openly embrace the universal accessibility concept. Even today there remains resistance to widespread access on the part of elite and prestige-driven universities which measure their institutional success in ways that are often contradictory to growing public needs.

During the panel discussion there were many examples of the increasingly significant role that the community colleges have played in American higher education since the federal debates nearly forty years ago. This is particularly relevant since the public community college sector rarely receives the appropriate credit for the foundational role that it has played in responding to the nation's desire for widespread access.

In addition to the ongoing work of the public community college sector, it is also important to recognize that higher education in its collective capacity has been viewed in a different and more open light since the early 1990s. What most influenced the attitudinal shift from elitism to egalitarianism was a widespread acceptance of the need for a globally competitive knowledge-based economy. No longer were institutions simply viewed as cultural training grounds for young minds or as tools to advance individual economic opportunity. During this period a major transformation occurred in the way that governments viewed colleges and universities. National economic conditions became dependent on institutions of higher education as the primary vehicle to increase the stock of human capital and increase global competitiveness. Partially owing to the global relocation of manufacturing and other labor-intensive industries, national leaders rapidly began to better understand and acknowledge education as the key to developing knowledge-rich societies. Globalization has meant that education and human capital have become the true wealth of nations. Such modernization of understanding of wealth capacity has resulted in significant changes and emerging pressures on higher

education institutions. For example, the expansion of higher education systems in Western Europe during the last fifteen years has been
viewed by some as the most significant higher education development
in the last hundred years. According to *The Economist* (1997), the
victory of the concept of universal higher education over the old elitist
models that permeated much of the OECD world was the most important and 'the biggest single change in higher education over the last
two decades'. Unlike in previous decades, governments of today are
increasingly looking to the different higher education sectors to
augment learning skills and improve workers' ability to develop and
use new technology, thus enhancing productivity and strengthening
the state's economic position. According to Marshall (1995), former
Secretary of Labor in the Clinton Administration, 'Education is the
critical element in this transformational process. It can no longer be
considered apart from the state's overall economic strategies.' It is this
transformation to an increasing reliance on higher education as a principal economic engine in today's world economy which is changing
national economic and social needs more rapidly than ever before.

This important transformation was further evidenced in the findings
of the national report initiated by the Secretary of Education Margaret
Spellings and conducted by the Commission for the Future of Higher
Education (2006). The report states that 'America's national capacity
for excellence, innovation and leadership in higher education will be
central to our ability to sustain economic growth and social cohesive-
ness. Our colleges and universities will be a key source of the human
and intellectual capital needed to increase workforce productivity and
growth.' The report further observes that 'the transformation of the
world economy increasingly demands a more highly educated workforce with postsecondary education skills and credentials'. This report
highlights the growing reliance that is now being placed on the nation's
colleges and universities. Additionally, however, the report points out
the obvious fact that as the importance of higher education to a
nation's well-being increases, so too will the public scrutiny and
demand for greater productivity and accountability.

This significant trend toward reliance on higher education in the
eyes of governments has also accelerated the demands and pressures
faced by US colleges and universities. Since the early 1990s, many com-
petitor nations have adopted aggressive strategies and policies which
have created widespread access to higher education. Nations that once
trailed the United States in the percentage of students attending higher

education institutions and students completing their degrees have now surpassed it. According to recent data from the Organisation for Economic Co-operation and Development (OECD), the USA now ranks twelfth worldwide among major industrialized countries in higher education attainment with another dozen nations rapidly closing the existing gaps. With regard to accessibility to higher education institutions, where the USA led the world in the 1960s and 1970s, it has now fallen to thirteenth in bachelor's degrees and to tenth in access to master's degrees.

Numerous additional reports also have highlighted this disturbing global competitiveness picture. These international trends have effectively exacerbated the demands placed on colleges and universities by governments and businesses in their race for more aggressive economic systems. It also is anticipated that this competitive stress will intensify in the decades to come as the desire to create and acquire enriched human talent will become even more important for economic success.

## COLLEGE COSTS AND PRICING: WHO PAYS?

The second macro theme or issue that received significant attention from the presidential panel was the issue of college costs and institutional pricing behavior. The rising demand for higher education has caused governments to seek to shift larger portions of the costs of higher education to the student by raising user fees or student tuition. This issue was considered in great detail by the panel of presidents and a variety of perspectives were presented regarding the challenges associated with this realization. This single issue, the increased shifting of costs to the student, was the primary reason for the inquiry by the National Commission on the Cost of Higher Education in 1997. This commission was the precursor to the Spellings Commission that would be convered nearly a decade later. Unfortunately, the 1997 Commission ultimately failed miserably and played little role in changing any of the public's cost-related concerns about higher education. In fact, the official conclusion of this Commission was that the student tuition and fee issue needed more research instead of greater government scrutiny. Nearly a decade later, the Commission on the Future of Higher Education was convened by the Secretary of Education Margaret Spellings to tackle this and other issues that were left unresolved in

1997. The issue of how much of the cost of higher education should be borne by the student remains the prominent concern not only among individual states but nationally. The role that this issue plays in relation to other concerns such as accountability, expenditure escalation, and the lack of transparency of information for students, parents and taxpayers has also become a national priority.

The issue of cost sharing, which has become one of the most challenging higher education topics worldwide, is particularly tricky in a nation such as the United States for a number of reasons highlighted by the presidential panel during the forum. First, despite being one of the wealthiest nations on earth, our public resources are stretched very thin because of the wars in Iraq and Afghanistan and other expensive commitments to an aging American population. The irony of this position is that, despite discovering that the world has changed dramatically and higher education is now a driving force in terms of dictating that change, we do not want to recognize that enhanced public investment is needed, and indeed essential, if we are to succeed in developing the kind of knowledge-based society needed in the twenty-first century. This interesting confluence has people and policy makers focusing on higher education, however, many traditional, conservative voices still lack the political will and are too reluctant to commit new resources to educate the number of engineers, scientists and nurses needed by society. This is further evidenced by the flattening of the budgets of the National Institutes of Health (NIH) and the National Science Foundation (NSF), which show little indication of increasing in the near future.

Additionally, for many decades the issue of 'who pays, and who benefits' has been a hotly contested topic in the United States. This issue has been complicated by the persistent question that has plagued higher education for many decades regarding whether the enterprise is more a public good or private benefit. In the United States there is no clear answer to this question. Currently, we have 50 differing higher education finance systems and, while some states have very decentralized governance structures, many other states are highly decentralized. States are very inconsistent with regard to the issue of cost sharing; some states, such as Vermont, Pennsylvania and Colorado, have become student tuition and fee financed with only a very limited amount of public commitment or tax effort, while other states charge limited student tuition and fees and have much stronger common or public support. Unfortunately, this issue is further complicated by the fact that the federal government, which originally was viewed as a source to provide supplemental funding for higher education, is now responsible for providing more total revenues than all the states for postsecondary education. In 2005–06 federally supported grants, loans and tax credits constituted over $90 billion in revenues to students and higher education institutions, while aggregated state funding to higher education totaled $85 billion (*The Chronicle of Higher Education Almanac*, 2006).

To further complicate the student cost issue, the presidential panel also expressed varying perspectives and practices regarding the issue of student tuition and fees. For private universities like Vanderbilt or quasi-private universities like Cornell, setting institutional tuition and fee rates is an institutional decision that occurs annually to address growth in fixed costs and competitive educational expenditures with peer universities.

For many prestigious private universities, raising student tuition and fee rates has become an essential strategy to maintain competitive faculty salaries with peers in attempting to create for their institutions a market advantage over other universities. Numerous researchers have studied this issue in great detail and found that this development has placed public universities at a considerable disadvantage against their private peers (Alexander, 2003; Ehrenberg, 2002; Hearn, 2006). However, for public sector colleges and universities rising student tuition and fee rates are much more a consequence of limited state appropriations and reductions in state tax support. As states have reduced their commitments to public higher education institutions, colleges and universities have been forced to turn to student tuition and fees to respond to rising fixed costs, faculty salary increases, instructional staffing expenditures, and the other basic educational expenditures.

Considerable concern was also expressed by the presidents that the public frequently overestimates the average student tuition and fee rates, resulting in a misperception regarding what most students actually pay for their college education. This misperception has been fueled by the high-profile nature of a small number of high-cost institutions and a national press that often focuses on private elite institutions in the northeastern United States or on public flagship universities which are the highest-cost public sector institutions. Rarely does the full story about what an average student pays to attend college nationwide make its way to the front page. For example, public community colleges and comprehensive universities, where over 65 percent of America's higher education students are enrolled, are rarely mentioned in the national debates regarding student tuition and fee escalation. In fact, the average student tuition and fee rate for a college attendee today is only around $4000 annually. This is considerably less than the $40 000 of the often publicized highest cost private sector institutions or the $20 000 of the average private higher education institution, or even the $6000 of the average public university nationwide.

To better inform the public it is important to provide greater transparency of information regarding college costs and expenditure rates to the multiple constituency groups. This is one of the recommendations advocated by the Spellings Commission and would most likely help students and parents better understand the complex nature of college costs. It would also provide much better information about which colleges and universities have been more successful than others in keeping their costs affordable and expenditures under control.

Unfortunately, however, in this context there appeared to be general consensus that this troubling fiscal trend would continue throughout higher education. In fact, as observed by Chancellor William Kirwan (2006) one year earlier at a similar forum, 'clearly, what we are facing is not a period of growing public investment in higher education. We are instead witnessing a systemic and sustained disinvestment in higher education at the federal, state, and local levels. And this is certainly more than a short term trend.' Kirwan further observed that 'the disinvestment trend has accelerated in recent years owing to rising health care and energy costs, and mandated spending for K-12 education'. Moreover, it has been higher education which has suffered the most and borne the brunt of difficult state budgetary periods, since it is only a discretionary part of most state budgets. Legislatures also have increasingly viewed higher education as having fall-back options in the form of student tuition and fees.

In this regard, during the forum I advanced two policy-based recommendations designed both to stabilize state appropriations for higher education and to slow down escalating student tuition and fee rates. First, federal policymakers should design and support a program that provides incentives to states to maintain their tax support of public institutions – maintenance of effort. It would not be beyond the appropriate reach of federal policy to establish a threshold of state tax effort for public higher education as measured by state support per student. Such a policy could provide matching resources to states that maintained above-average effort for their systems. In measuring support through state tax effort, which takes into account a state's wealth capacity, the federal government can develop more helpful assistance policies. When one reviews current per student expenditures by state, it is interesting to note that some poorer states may generally have higher tax effort and support while correspondingly having lower student tuition and fees. This policy would provide rewards or incentives to encourage states to maintain higher tax support for higher education, which would eliminate the primary reason for rapid college and university tuition and fee increases in the public sector.

The precedent for this kind of federal policy for states is found in a similar initiative adopted in the Educational Amendments of 1972, which augmented the federal Higher Education Act of 1965, when the State Student Incentive Program (SSIG), currently known as the Leveraging Educational Assistance Partnership (LEAP) program was set up. The intent of this Act was to encourage states to support and implement state direct student aid programs; in this case, matching federal funds flow to institutions in states that have met federal requirements to initiate and finance state direct student aid programs. Currently LEAP has been so effective in achieving its original purpose that policymakers have since considered eliminating the program because of the pull on federal resources in order to redirect these funds to more essential programs.

The second policy recommendation is already being considered by the federal government and mandates that all institutions, both public and private, submit their 'net tuition' or average cost of attendance, instead of their 'sticker prices', to the federal government and the public at large. This would provide more useful information to students and parents regarding the average rate that a student actually pays to attend an institution annually. This policy also would allow institutions to provide greater accountability and transparency regarding their pricing structures and systems.

Unless we begin to develop new strategies and public policies that creatively address the issue of student cost sharing or increasing tuition and fees, little will be done to remedy the current trends that have plagued the public's perception of higher education. By working to stabilize the manner in which states provide public funding to higher education institutions, we have an opportunity to effectively address the primary problem that impacts nearly 75 percent of the student population who reside in all public colleges and universities.

## ACCOUNTABILITY AND PUBLIC SCRUTINY

The third macro theme to emerge from the panel discussion encompasses the evolving world of public accountability. As public scrutiny intensifies over the issue of college costs and most states have come to the realization that successful knowledge-based economies are grounded in the quality and accessibility of strong educational systems for all citizens, government authorities are no longer as receptive to the traditional self-regulatory processes that have dominated higher education development for many years. The issue of increased accountability extends well beyond the concerns about student tuition and fees. Increasingly, public officials and consumers want to know which institutions are educating their students well and offering high 'value-added' opportunities. The public also want to know which institutions are being efficient in the expenditure of public resources and providing the most educational value with those resources.

This topic has always raised considerable concern for many private higher education institutions and some public community colleges. Private colleges and universities have always been very reluctant to embrace new forms of government accountability, while public community colleges have expressed concern that, because they provide a wide array of educational programs to multiple constituencies, they cannot fully measure their effectiveness or success. For many community college leaders, using gross measures of student retention and graduation rates to gauge an institution's effectiveness is very problematic.

However, when measuring value-added educational outcomes, there seems to be a degree of interest that might support further inquiry into this arena. As long as the educational outcomes are assessed as true value-added measurements taking into account the complex mission of public higher education institutions which remain committed to their public missions and foundations, then most institutions which primarily serve lower-income students could come out of the process looking very effective.

The panel also advocated that any new federal or state accountability measures or directives should be carefully constructed with the involvement of higher education leaders and experts and that it should reflect the desirable diversity of the American higher education. If developed appropriately, these decisions to make our colleges and universities more accountable could prove effective in winning back some of the public's trust for decades to come. Despite some of the initial concerns regarding increased public accountability and scrutiny, it was perceived by the presidents that a more centralized demand for greater accountability will be inevitable and require more attention in the future for all institutions. What is apparent is that this trend will only intensify in the years to come, primarily because of society's growing educational appetite and the economic need to remain globally competitive.

## PHILANTHROPY

The fourth and final macro theme that was discussed in great detail by the panel of presidents was the enterprise of philanthropy. When calculating the amount of time that was spent cultivating and generating private donations and revenues, the presidents estimated that they spent between 20 and 35 percent of their time on philanthropic endeavors. The increased need to generate private resources by college and university presidents has become an essential part of a campus leader's role because these funds help to meet essential campus needs, enhance areas of university distinction, and provide flexible funds for multiple purposes. What is increasingly apparent is that, to whatever extent possible, institutions should aggressively look to diversify their revenue streams and secure non-state sources. Even though these funds should not be viewed as 'substitution' funds, such revenue can complement public funding and enhance the ability of institutions to achieve their educational missions and goals. Presidents in all sectors are being asked not only to build private endowments but to develop consistent streams of private revenues that can be used for a variety of restricted and unrestricted educational purposes. Even public community college presidents have entered this new arena and two-year institutions throughout the nation are in the process of developing comprehensive fundraising operations and offices.

## CONCLUSION

Within the last two decades higher education in the USA and many other economically advanced nations has matured in ways previously unseen in our civilization. Driven by a 'new economic dynamic', societies throughout the world are requiring an ever changing combination of highly skilled human capital and knowledge that only education can provide. Therefore, the current challenges facing colleges and universities most likely will not be temporary and will require institutions to be able to define and demonstrate educational objectives and achievements in more utilitarian terms. Institutions that are unable to define and demonstrate their worth in more practical ways will have limited success in meeting the new demands being placed on higher education.

According to Hearn (2006, pp. 38–9), 'the challenge lies in identifying danger. The risks to essential traditions and values in higher education may lie more in the cumulative effects of seemingly minor, necessary, and attractive adaptations than in obvious radical reforms'. This statement encapsulates many of the concerns expressed by the presidential panel. How do college and university presidents predict the future? Or, more importantly, how do college and university presidents position their institutions to succeed as individual campuses while also collectively serving the greater needs of society?

The four principal themes discussed in this chapter are not new to academic administrators nor will they fade from the higher education landscape at some time in the near future. Greater societal expectations, rising college costs, increased accountability, and identification of alternative revenue streams are all important issues that will continue to play significant roles in our ability as colleges and universities to better serve our students and society. This is the price we must pay for our success and future progress.

# REFERENCES

Alexander, F.K. (2003), 'Comparative study of state tax effort and the role of federal government policy in shaping revenue reliance patterns', in F.K. Alexander and R.G. Ehrenberg (eds), *Maximizing Revenue in Higher Education*, (New Directions for Institutional Research, 119), San Francisco: Jossey-Bass, pp. 13–26.

Applebome, P. (2007), 'Rethinking the path to prestige', *The New York Times*, 29 April.

Ehrenberg, R. (2002), *Tuition Rising: Why College Costs So Much*, Cambridge, MA: Harvard University Press.

Hearn, T. (2006), 'Enhancing revenues at colleges and universities', in R. Clark and M. d'Ambrosio (eds), *The New Balancing Act in the Business of Higher Education*, Cheltenham, UK and Northampton, MA, USA: Edward Elgar, p. 46.

Kirwan, William (2006), 'Higher education: meeting today's challenges and regaining the public's trust', in R. Clark and M. d'Ambrosio (eds), *The New Balancing Act in the Business of Higher Education*, Cheltenham, UK and Northampton, MA, USA: Edward Elgar, p. 46.

Marshall, R. (1995), 'The global jobs crisis', *Foreign Policy: The Global Jobs Crisis*, Washington, DC: The Carnegie Endowment for International Peace.

Mortenson, T. (2007), 'The gated communities of higher education: 50 most exclusive public and private 4-year institutions FY 1994 to FY 2005', *Postsecondary Education Opportunity*, 177.

*The Chronicle of Higher Education Almanac* (2006), Washington, DC.

*The Economist* (1997), 'A survey of universities: the knowledge factory', 4–10 October, pp. 4–8.

# 2. Strengthening the academic presidency: recommendations for presidents and governing boards

**Robert M. O'Neil**

Shortly before the TIAA-CREF Institute convened the conference, Transformational Change in Higher Education, the Association of Governing Boards (AGB) released the report of its Task Force on the State of the Presidency in American Higher Education. The title of the report, *The Leadership Imperative*, clearly signaled its central theme. At the outset, the Task Force 'contends that a new style of collaborative but decisive leadership – integral leadership – is the key to addressing [the most daunting issues facing contemporary higher education]'. Integral leadership, continued the executive summary, 'succeeds in fulfilling the multiple, disparate strands of presidential responsibility, and conceives of these responsibilities as parts of a coherent whole'.

Such leadership, in essence, links the major academic constituencies 'in a well-functioning partnership purposefully devoted to a well-defined, broadly affirmed institutional vision'. Some 43 specific recommendations spelled out the import of such bold declarations – desirable actions addressed respectively to governing boards, to presidents, to state policymakers, and to AGB itself. The attention of university boards was specifically drawn to the most pertinent and sensitive areas of trustee responsibility – supporting presidential leadership, conducting a presidential search, presidential evaluation and compensation, board accountability, and presidential renewal and succession.

Had there been any uncertainty about the timeliness of the Task Force's mission when the group convened in the fall of 2005, not the slightest doubt remained when the time came for issuance of the report a year later. Indeed, the intervening 12 months may well have been the very worst of times for the academic presidency and for the governing boards that were most directly affected. The widely publicized failures of presidencies at Harvard, American, Case-Western and Indiana Universities might have been clearly the most visible of such misadventures, but these were surely not the only institutions to suffer from leadership breakdowns during the year. Not only were the governing boards of those universities directly and profoundly affected while the Task Force deliberated; unprecedented divisions and deep public embarrassment would during this time face governing boards that sought either to support an existing embattled president or, as in the cases of Gallaudet University and the University of Iowa, to secure new leadership in a divided and unsettled context. It would be hard to imagine a year during which the need would emerge more clearly for just the sort of guidance and counsel the Task Force would provide to the American academic community.

This group revisited issues that had occupied a predecessor Task Force a decade earlier. Not only was there valuable continuity in the pivotal role of AGB as the convener of both groups, providing vital staff support on both occasions, but the Association's former president, Richard T. Ingram, returned as a member of the second project. Two outside members who had served on the earlier Task Force also accepted reappointment in 2005. Cornell University President Frank H.T. Rhodes had retired from that office by the time the later group convened, but brought to the new task an invaluable mix of administrative experience both in the Ivy League and at the University of Michigan, blending public and private perspectives.

## TASK FORCE LEADERSHIP AND STRUCTURE

Perhaps the clearest sense of symmetry came in the role of former Virginia Governor Gerald L. Baliles, who chaired and guided both studies. As an interesting sidelight, during the year the later group deliberated, he became for the first time a senior university administrator, as the new Director of the University of Virginia's Miller Center of Public Affairs. And since the primary focus of the Miller Center is the Presidency of the United States, this new assignment could hardly have better suited the needs of the successor Task Force. The balance of the 2005–06 roster included a distinguished group of presidents and chancellors, present and former, of institutions both public and private, joined by three seasoned trustees (also both public and independent) and the presidents of the American Council on Education and the Education Commission of the States. Such a distinguished and varied panel generated high expectations, which the release of the report in the fall of 2006 would not in the least disappoint.

The panel that agreed to address challenges to the academic presidency at the November 2006 TIAA-CREF Institute conference included three people who had played central roles in shaping *The Leadership Imperative* – Governor Baliles, AGB President Richard D. Legon, and Drexel University Trustee Harold W. Pote. They were joined by two seasoned administrators – Pitzer College President Laura Skandera Trombley and Norfolk State University Executive Vice President Alvin J. Schexnider. Each panelist brought his or her special insight and experience to the discussion, thus blending public and private higher education perspectives in ways that such gatherings do not always manage to do. Each member of the panel responded to specific questions as they arose within the panel and, at the close of the session, to inquiries and suggestions offered by a keenly engaged audience that had patiently awaited the opportunity for their participation. While the catalyst for this conference session was unmistakably the recent release of *The Leadership Imperative*, the discussion was in no sense constrained by the deliberations of the Task Force or by its conclusions. The audience participation, in fact, broadened the discussion by introducing a couple of issues that had received less emphasis in *The Leadership Imperative* but were quite germane to the conference and to the current concern about university leadership.

## DYNAMICS OF THE BOARD–PRESIDENT RELATIONSHIP

Not surprisingly, given both the title and the central theme of the Task Force report, it was the complex and sensitive relationship between board and president that drew the greatest amount of time and attention at this session. If there was universal agreement on any conclusion, it would be the indisputable need to make that dynamic truly collaborative. Recognizing that governing boards do not always provide the optimal degree and type of support for a president, even in relatively tranquil times, AGB President Richard Legon recalled some poignant accounts the Task Force had heard of presidents who had been essentially 'orphaned' by their boards – 'they're hired; they are told to do well and conquer and follow the strategic plan, and then the board maybe steps back too far'.

The opposite relationship seemed equally inimical to the goal of productive collaboration – (again in Legon's words) 'boards that are overly engaged and overly aggressive, if not internally then sometimes externally with the constituents outside the institution'. What everyone at this session, most especially the panelists, seemed to agree was most urgently needed (if not always familiar to trustees from non-academic backgrounds) was a happy mean between the unengaged board that 'orphaned' its president and the intrusive/aggressive board that smothered or preempted its campus leadership. The central challenge that faced this session, especially the panel, was how to achieve such a balanced relationship in the demanding context of rapidly evolving and highly stressed university governance. Norfolk State University's Alvin Schexnider emphasized the centrality of 'open dialogue' between president and board, underscoring his conviction that 'the issue of integrity . . . has to permeate every facet of the relationship'. Governor Baliles may have put it best as he framed this goal: 'I can't imagine a president being successful and having any longevity at an institution of higher learning without having a good working collaborative relationship with the board.' Several responsive themes defined and shaped most of the rest of the discussion during this session.

### 'Integral Leadership' at the Core

Central to such desirable balance is the concept of integral leadership, which Governor Baliles early in the session described as one 'in which a president exerts a presence that is purposeful and consultative, deliberative yet decisive, and capable of course corrections as new challenges emerge'. Yet such a presidential role can hardly flourish without support and understanding from the board – requiring a greater awareness than most new trustees might bring to the board that the academic presidency is (in Laura Skandera Trombley's words) 'an extraordinarily stressful position . . . one that never stops'. The need for board support flows directly from this reality, which the academic leaders in the group continued to emphasize. Thus there may be times when a president speaks out boldly, ruffles some feathers and, in Richard Legon's assessment, 'the board needs to be strong and say to those members of the community, "This is the choice we made, this person is going to be excellent, and I want you to know that it's time for the community to rally behind him (or her)."'

Supporting the president was, however, seen by the panel as much more than an abstract or generalized commitment. Throughout this session, the occasions on which such support was vital to a president's success or even survival emerged in very specific dimensions. First of all, of course, there was a need for great care and commitment on the board's part in selecting a new campus leader. Late in the session, former Kent State University President Carol Cartwright stressed a vital if often neglected dimension of board responsibility at this stage of the process – to ensure that a candidate for the presidency displays not just 'leadership and good management' but also a genuine 'calling to this extraordinary opportunity in leadership'. Drexel Trustee Hal Pote readily concurred, adding his belief that prospective presidents must 'have a real passion . . . for higher education and for that school', ready to reach out to the community 'and make the case that [higher education] is one of the true drivers of healthy economic growth and the culture of our country'.

The clear import of such statements could hardly be mistaken or undervalued. If a board engaged in a presidential search settles for less, and appoints someone who lacks such 'passion' and a sense of 'calling', then (in Pote's words again) it 'probably [has chosen] the wrong person, who may well fail on some other counts'. Not only is the non-passionate candidate who has thus been selected now placed at a potentially severe disadvantage in terms of his own prospects for success in office, but also, even more serious, the institution risks having to suffer lackluster and indifferent leadership at the one time in its history when a clear and firm commitment should be expected.

### Choosing and Welcoming a New President

The process of selecting and placing in office a new president obligates the governing board to provide and enhance other measures of support. Once the appointment has been made, this panel agreed, it is the board's duty to explain to relevant stakeholders and constituents the rationale for the selection and to articulate the expectations the board holds for those who will be working with and for the new president. A major potential contribution of a caring board lies in facilitating a smooth transition as the new president arrives and assumes office. Indeed, Laura Skandera Trombley recalled her own salutary experience in being greeted and oriented by a board-created transition committee of faculty, staff, administrators and a few trustees, with whom she met and from whom she received valuable guidance even before arriving on campus, and to whom she turned with greater benefit after she had taken office. She urged a wider consideration and, where possible, replication of such a structure – 'an extremely positive process [which] also brought the board into the community in a much more thoughtful way than typically happens'.

Another vital role that boards can and should play in facilitating a smooth transition is to cushion or protect an incoming president (in so far as possible) from the potentially adverse external publicity and internal distrust or hostility likely to result from unavoidable expenditures. Drexel Trustee Hal Pote noted that 'every time you hire a new president, some things are going to pop up in the newspaper'. Illustratively, Norfolk State University Executive Vice President Alvin Schexnider recalled that, when he was serving as interim president, he saw to it that a much needed renovation of the president's house was completed 'on my watch so that when the new president came, that was not an issue for her with the newspaper'. Thus a wise interim administrator 'took the spears', as he put it, and graciously incurred the public wrath that was likely to accompany an unavoidable expenditure. The incoming president was undoubtedly appreciative, not only to find habitable quarters awaiting her and her family but also to find herself beyond reach of potentially hostile media attention. Schexnider, meanwhile, appreciated with unusual sensitivity from his several relevant perspectives the critical need for 'the full board to understand the implications of a transition that may go awry' and to take such appropriate cautionary steps.

**Board Concern for a President's General Welfare**

Despite the more highly visible nature of the president's public and official role, discussion of the value of strong board support was by no means confined to that aspect of the job. Indeed, a board's duty to provide such official and public support was all but taken for granted by the panel and others who offered comments. What received far greater emphasis was the private or off-stage dynamic of presidential life. Following Laura Skandera Trombley's characterization of the presidency as 'an extraordinarily stressful position . . . that never stops', a vital though often neglected dimension of board–president relations emerged as the imperative of the human dimension, in which the board cares genuinely for the welfare of the president and his or her family. There seemed to be a clear consensus around the special value of (again in Trombley's words) recognizing that 'the board really needs to sit down and have a conversation with the [incoming] president about what is going on in terms of their personal life, as far as it concerns time for renewal, time for family, time for rest' – a board obligation to 'make sure that the presidents take care of themselves'.

### The Board Chair's Special Role

Although such responsibility for the president's personal health and welfare is one that all trustees share, this was one task that seemed to fall especially on the board's chair. For this and other reasons, Drexel Trustee Hal Pote observed at one point that 'the selection of the board chair is almost as important as the selection of the CEO'. President Laura Trombley concurred, adding that 'you need to have a strong board chair'. Governor Baliles, stressing the same theme, later added his belief that, 'if there's a good working relationship between the president and the board chair', such critical needs as managing 'the personal health of and pressures on the president' are far likelier to receive the attention they deserve in a collaborative institution.

The immense value of having a supportive board chair emerged in one especially poignant and appealing dynamic. Along the way, even the most successful president will face unfamiliar challenges for which the guidance of a seasoned senior colleague could be invaluable, although not easy to find and possibly awkward to pursue. A compassionate board chair should, in Richard Legon's view, be especially well positioned to 'make clear to this first-time president that "you ought to have a group of mentors – people who have been through it" ', adding that 'not only is it OK to say, "I'd like to have some help and some advice", but "Let me make a phone call for you and introduce you to someone like that and please avail yourself of that." ' While this responsibility falls broadly under the rubric of 'board support for the president', it particularly engages the board chair as that one trustee for whom providing such deeply personal and sensitive guidance attains special meaning and import.

## Evaluation and Assessment

Another highly desirable, if not routinely observed, dimension of board–president relations involves evaluation and assessment. The panel agreed that in a healthy relationship the president should be ready to ask, and the board ready to answer, even fairly early questions inviting informal appraisal, such as 'How am I doing? I know I don't have a performance review for another six months, but what are you hearing? What can I do better?' The premise of so open and candid a relationship was another element on which there was clear consensus in this session – the value of early negotiation by the board and the president of performance goals and objectives by which the president would be assessed, along with clear desiderata for the board's own performance. Especially relevant to both aspects of that dynamic was the importance of a strategic planning process in which board and president are fully and mutually engaged. Such a process, in Drexel Trustee Hal Pote's view, provides the essential template for performance appraisal – specifically, because strategic planning 'begins to drive everyone in the right direction and it allows the board the opportunity to judge the performance of the senior team and for the board to judge its own performance'.

## Strategic Planning

In Trustee Pote's experience, in fact, the differences between planning in business and in the academy seemed 'very minimal'; Drexel's most recent five-year plan seemed to him 'the best strategic plan that I've seen in all my business career'. Drawing upon his extensive business experience and his trusteeship, Pote concluded his appraisal of the academic planning process with this telling observation:

> It's hard work putting those [plans] together because it involves a lot of conversation and a lot of give and take on the front end; it's not just about what we want to be, it's about what we are not going to be. And I do believe

that in the academic world, telling folks where we are not going to invest our resources is a critical and often contentious issue.

Pote and others on this panel were impressed by the potential of the planning process to exemplify the concept of integral leadership, in ways that were of course quite germane to the focus of the session.

## Easing the Outbound as well as the Inbound Transition

Finally, and inevitably, at the end of the 'life cycle of the presidency', shared attention must be given to that time of transition as well. One often recalls in this vein President Clark Kerr's quip on the day in January 1967 when the University of California Board of Regents terminated his appointment: 'I left office exactly as I entered it – fired with enthusiasm!' This conference, reflecting wise counsel from the Task Force, saw the conclusion of a presidential term somewhat more sensitively. Whether the passage is smooth or stormy, the institution's welfare must transcend any personal considerations on the part of either president or trustees.

Relatively little has been said about the ending of the cycle, the sensitive dynamic between successor and predecessor, and the like. One commentator from the audience ventured that 'The behavior of the ex-President can have a huge impact – particularly a popular one who knows all the trustees – on the likes of the current president.' The special challenge that emerged from this discussion was how to handle 'a popular ex-president who remains on campus', as many are likely to do unless they move on to a senior administrative post elsewhere. Laura Skandera Trombley offered her perspective as one who had observed and worried about 'institutions where presidents can't stop being presidents'.

When the presence of such a revered former administrator creates a 'ripple effect for the current president' – especially when the predecessor remains on the board or holds other potentially undermining roles – 'the institution needs to be protected, and that's the role of the board', which may in such a situation 'need to really step in and make sure that everybody understands the rules of engagement'. AGB's Richard Legon added his belief that it is often 'a mistake for the retiring president or CEO to remain as a part of the community'; instead, 'for a lot of reasons . . . it is much better for that person to depart from the premises'. He noted that the Task Force report addressed this precise issue and gave specific attention to the sensitivity needed 'when the presidency is brought to a conclusion'.

## PUBLIC VERSUS PRIVATE: TWO DISTINCT SPHERES

Although not a major theme of the conference, the contrast between independent and state-supported institutions was an inescapable reality. Some of the differences between sectors are obvious – notably, that most private boards control their own appointments, while public trustees are typically selected by a state governor, usually with the concurrence of a legislative body. Public boards are also subject to vastly greater scrutiny than are most of their private counterparts, and incur various legal obligations and burdens that the independent sector is largely spared. Yet this superficially clear distinction has always been somewhat blurred in practice – not only by the presence of 'hybrid' institutions like Cornell and Alfred which contain both public and private academic units, but also by such anomalies as the Federal Land Grant status of MIT and Brown, or the presence of ex officio public officials on the boards of Yale, Tulane and Dartmouth.

Indeed, the late James O. Freedman, who had extensive presidential experience on both sides of this divide, noted that 'One of the major strengths of the Dartmouth board was the fact that the Governor of New Hampshire, by prescription of the 1769 charter from King George III, was an ex officio member.' Moreover, the primacy of alumni as trustees might seem an exclusive attribute of the private sector, though Indiana's public boards contain elected alumni trustees, and by statute Virginia's governor is to receive a roster of potential board candidates from each of several of the Commonwealth's public universities' alumni associations before making new board appointments – though the laws make clear that the governor's selection process is not confined to the alumni list.

Perhaps most unsettling to the traditional notion of a public–private dichotomy is the emerging of so-called privatization at certain highly selective state universities with unusual flexibility in setting tuition charges. A process that began over a decade ago with the law and business schools at the Universities of Michigan and

Virginia has now reached more broadly, and to some observers may even offer a viable alternative to legislative support for much of the public sector. Yet, as Cornell University Professor Ronald Ehrenberg wisely cautioned in his 2006 Howard Bowen Lecture at Iowa, such privatization really works only for the most selective of the publics, and even there 'special efforts will be required to make sure that they continue to enroll students from lower- and middle-income families'.

As for the rest of the public sector, Ehrenberg notes, '[P]rivatization is much less likely to be a viable strategy for our nation's public comprehensives and two-year colleges.' Indeed, even in Ann Arbor and Charlottesville, what works for law and business does not extend to education, nursing, or social work – or even to much of the arts and sciences. Suffice it to say that some of the public sector partakes increasingly of a 'private' character, while most of the state-supported sector will remain just that.

While the public–private distinction importantly shaped much of the discussion at the conference, as well as the content of the Task Force report, the precise issues that drew most attention seemed to reflect shared interests and concerns – areas in which the dynamics of board–president relations transcended the affiliation of the institution. The counsel that emerged from the conference in many dimensions should in fact prove equally useful to the independent and the state-supported institution. Indeed, such commonalities may have surprised many of the participants – as much as they had earlier impressed members of the Task Force, drawn as they had been almost equally from the two sectors, and chaired by a state governor who had also served his own private alma mater (Wesleyan University) through membership on its governing board.

## ROLES AND RESPONSIBILITIES OF TRUSTEES

The second major theme of this session on the academic presidency was the roles and responsibilities of trustees themselves. A central premise of this discussion was a sense of rapid change in the character of trusteeship – a need to recognize the substantially broader and more complex responsibilities that board service entails in the twenty-first century. President Laura Skandera Trombley noted that 'the nature of trusteeship has changed enormously', in part because of the 'public demand for greater transparency'. Thus, she continued, 'trustees now have larger responsibilities not just in terms of their fiduciary oversight, but also for [the strategic planning process]'.

Governor Baliles promptly concurred with this assessment, but added a hopeful note – that 'the combination of circumstances [affecting trusteeship] in our public arena' seemed to him to have brought about 'increasing cooperation between board members and the presidents' as institutions respond to such heightened pressures. But the discussion during this session left no doubt that the participants fully shared an appreciation of the escalating responsibilities and obligations facing those who agree to serve on college and university governing boards.

**Trustee Selection**

Not surprisingly, the process of trustee selection received substantial attention. Although the panel did not include a public university trustee, Governor Baliles' perspective fortuitously reflected both sectors; noting that he had served on the Wesleyan board, he drew from his Virginia gubernatorial experience some fascinating insights into the appointive process. Before selecting new trustees, he found it most helpful to analyze the institution's particular needs, a process that involved consultation with current trustees and the president of each institution. He then sought board candidates who 'understood that managing and running a higher education institution these days is a very complex enterprise'. Interestingly, Governor Baliles felt strongly that he should not interview prospective board appointees themselves because 'I did not want them to feel beholden to me because I made the appointment.'

The Governor also drew from his experience as a legislator and as Attorney General ample exposure to the corrosive presence of 'political appointees' on public boards – a situation that, in his own selections, 'I was resolved to avoid'. Later he cited Virginia's salutary experience with an unusual if not unique screening panel for public sector board selection – an addition that enhanced measurably the quality of service on Virginia's public university boards. Norfolk State's Alvin Schexnider, drawing in part on his own experience as a Virginia State University trustee, lauded this process, which in his view 'has helped enormously to improve the caliber, the leadership on the board . . . and will continue the current direction'. Near the close of the session, AGB's Richard Legon revisited this issue, adding his own view that 'Virginia is really the shining star that we take around the country to try to show what a non-partisan selection process can bring to the table in terms of choosing primarily on merit as opposed to other alternatives.'

### Trustee Performance Appraisal – and Concluding Appointments

At the other end of the life cycle of trusteeship, the session also considered the challenge of easing unproductive (or even counterproductive) trustees off the board, particularly in the private sector. There was general agreement that performance goals and periodic appraisal are essential not only for presidents but quite as much for governing boards. President Laura Skandera Trombley cited to this end Pitzer's practice of initiating such appraisal in the second year of a trustee's three-year term, in order 'to determine if they will be offered a second three-year term'. Drexel Trustee Hal Pote developed this theme, applauding rigorous board self-assessment, but recognizing that 'the hardest issue obviously is always inviting somebody to leave [a governing board]'. The only honest approach to that unwelcome task, he insisted, is for a board chair to say, 'Here's the end of your term. Here is what the assessment said.'

Such a drastic ultimatum can sometimes be avoided, Pote added in a more redemptive vein, 'if you start to give a board member feedback ahead of time that, "Hey, you're not engaging or you've fallen short of your giving goals, or you know you're felt to be disruptive" – and [with such guidance] give folks a chance to change whatever it is that's troublesome to the other board members or the president rather than just saying at the end of three years, "Thanks; it's been great."' Obviously the results of such a process will differ quite substantially between public and private university boards; what was striking about this discussion, as with many other parts of this session, was the parallel emphasis across both sectors on such practices as regular and rigorous board self-assessment, followed by prompt feedback and early intervention.

### Trustee Accountability – an AGB Imperative

The subject of trustee accountability also figured prominently in this session, and again reflected more similarities than differences between public and independent university boards. Accountability was a natural theme for this session, if only because the Task Force report called upon AGB to 'develop a statement on Board Accountability and Fiduciary Oversight that boards may use as a model'. Such a statement was already in the drafting process, headed for final approval by AGB's Board of Directors in mid-January 2007 – only the fourth such statement the Association's board has issued in its 86-year history. Happily, the approach to issues of accountability reflected at the TIAA-CREF Institute session conformed closely to discussions that were central to the framing of the AGB Statement. There was, for one thing, appreciation of the vital if elusive distinction between trustee responsibility and the more elusive and perhaps more subjective concept of accountability – essentially the standards and criteria by which society judges the performance of those who serve on academic governing boards.

Under the rubric of accountability, special attention focused on the board's fiduciary responsibility – in Richard Legon's words, 'a significant part of *The Leadership Imperative*'. The recently heightened emphasis on accountability reflected conditions in the larger society quite as much as forces or pressures that are distinctive to academic institutions – corporate financial scandals at Enron, Worldcom and elsewhere, and serious lapses in the integrity and governance of United Way and other quite visible non-profits, as well as highly publicized breakdowns in academic governance at American University and other universities within the past year or two. Thus the framing of such a statement on board accountability, and eventually securing its widespread acceptance across the academic community, had become a very high priority for AGB, and one that logically nurtured the quite timely discussion at the TIAA-CREF Institute conference.

This particular session reflected broad appreciation of the value of voluntary self-regulation at a time of societal skepticism and distrust. While few if any governing boards would relish subjecting themselves to heightened measures of accountability, a clear commitment to self-regulation almost certainly enhances the prospect for averting or reducing pressure for external regulation or government intervention. As Drexel Trustee Hal Pote put the case: 'I don't believe that additional laws and regulations are necessarily desirable, and I would urge that we all do what we can to avoid that by demonstrating that self-regulation can work.'

**Self-regulation and Fiscal Integrity**

The case of Sarbanes–Oxley offered an especially apt illustration. Although everyone in higher education recognizes that this rigorous federal financial reform legislation does not apply at all to the non-profit sector, and could not be adopted by a college or university even if it wished to do so, it contains analogous principles that may prove helpful to higher education. As President Trombley reported, Pitzer College has recently 'adapted many of the recommendations that Sarbanes–Oxley dictates' – creating for the first time a separate board audit committee, establishing 'a very transparent budgeting process [including] a committee where faculty and students sit along with administrators' and imposing a new requirement that every trustee in his or her first year on the board sit on the budget committee.

Drexel Trustee Hal Pote identified himself as 'one of the few people in the business world that's willing to say anything good about Sarbanes–Oxley', adding that, despite strong resistance in many quarters, 'much of it makes a lot of sense'. Drexel's board, like Pitzer's, had recently 'adapted what we thought were all of the relevant provisions of Sarbanes–Oxley that apply to a university'. Everyone who spoke to this issue recognized that Sarbanes–Oxley and its analogous implications for higher education were simply a proxy for the broader mandate of integrity at all levels, clearly the most central transcendent value, applicable as fully to public and private sector boards.

Behind adapting relevant provisions of Sarbanes–Oxley, and similar voluntary actions in areas to which legal mandates did not apply, Trustee Hal Pote envisioned a potentially new dimension of a private university board's broad accountability to myriad constituent interests – '[to] donors, past and present, the parents who are paying tuition, the kids who deserve an education, faculty that deserve a place to grow and develop'. Such recognition in turn yielded for a conscientious trustee this daunting rhetorical question: if a board starts with 'Who are your constituents, what is it that they rightfully look to this institution to provide and, therefore, as their fiduciaries, what is . . . the process by which I as a board member should determine that we are appropriately delivering to our constituents what they are rightfully owed?' Thus, while public and private university boards might well respond in very different ways to such a question, and would undoubtedly accord different priorities to such varied constituent interests, the question is surely one that trustees in both sectors need to address thoughtfully, with answers likely to guide the fulfillment of their respective governance roles.

## THE EXPANDING MISSION OF HIGHER EDUCATION

A final theme that drew recurrent interest from panelists and others at the session was the steadily broadening agenda of higher education, implicating both presidents and trustees. Drexel Trustee Hal Pote urged recognition of the need for academic leaders to bring to the job not only a deep pride in their own institutions, but also a 'passion' for higher education in general. Increasingly, he continued, 'the college president needs to step out with the support of the board and make the case that [higher education] is one of the true drivers of healthy economic growth and the culture of our country'. Pitzer President Trombley, in her closing comments, echoed the same theme: recalling *The Leadership Imperative*'s emphasis on encouraging more bold and courageous presidential expression, she underscored her own belief that 'presidents need to be vocal about things that are important to them and things that matter, and to use that pulpit'. At a time of growing anxiety on and off campus about incurring risk for almost anything that is said publicly or even posted on an obscure website, she observed that 'it's ever more important for higher education to consistently and clearly and constantly get this message out about the importance of higher education and not to let that fear dictate what you think and what you say'.

In his closing statement, Governor Baliles voiced his mounting concern about the future of academe in twenty-first century America. Uneasy about the capacity of the academic community to meet the mounting fiscal challenges of the new millennium, he stressed what seemed to him 'the need to speak collectively about the importance of intellectual capital and the ability of higher education to deliver it'. He concluded by sharing with conference participants his deepest worry: 'If higher education cannot speak with a voice that is compelling and concise, then higher education's financial stability is going to be in jeopardy.' That rather ominous prospect, said Richard Legon in closing the session, had to be 'the final word', one that most appropriately was conveyed by the chair of the Task Force that had produced *The Leadership Imperative*.

## A CONCLUDING PERSONAL PERSPECTIVE

While a rapporteur who could not attend the conference incurs a substantial disadvantage, anyone who has held administrative posts at several major public universities must welcome the tone and focus of discussion at this recent conference. Not only is there much reassurance in the central emphasis of the Task Force and the conference on the collaborative model of the 'Leadership Imperative', but the particular dimensions of that theme proved especially congenial, in addition to the remarkably high degree of concurrence on all the basic issues between the trustees and the active administrators who comprised the panel and the added comments from the audience toward the close of the session. The close attention given to the personal needs of a president or chancellor – from the moment of selection and installation to the close of a term of office – was heartening to anyone who has held such an office. The special concern for the ongoing day-to-day welfare of the president during a term, as well as the need for board guidance to a chief executive in seeking direction from a mentor, received far greater attention in 2006 than they would have garnered a decade earlier. In short, the striking recognition by all the conference participants (as well as by the Task Force) of the human and personal needs of a president touched a sympathetic nerve, and reflected a caring and compassionate perspective on all sides.

One who has served either as trustee or president would be naïve to dismiss the potential for occasional tension and even discord between those who govern a university and those who administer its day-to-day affairs. Neither the Task Force nor the conference participants could be faulted for any such naïveté. Yet their response to such reality, marking a central theme of the Task Force and of the conference, was that fundamental interests of American higher education transcend such differences and invite – indeed compel – making common cause to enhance a shared mission. That new emphasis on collaboration within the 'Leadership Imperative' reflected in substantial part the far more competitive global climate within which American higher education functions in the early twenty-first century. Yet the greatly heightened intensity of competition would not alone account fully for the keenly sensitive tone of these proceedings. Beyond external forces and pressures, this strikingly compassionate view of the presidency and board–president dynamics seems to have had deeper and quite indigenous roots. Quite simply, treating senior university administrators in so caring a mode is good business and good policy for all concerned.

# 3. Aligning institutional vision with policymakers' and the public's interests

**Patrick M. Callan**

This chapter explores the alignment of three extremely complex and moving parts: institutional vision, policymakers' interest, and the public's interest. This formidable task – and the title of this chapter – was assigned to one of several roundtable groups at the conference, Transformational Change in Higher Education: Positioning Your Institution for Future Success. The five members of the panel represented the diversity and complexity of American higher education, with the exception of community colleges. Their contributions on the problems and opportunities of alignment are presented here. To a substantial extent, these contributions reflect the institutional perspectives of the presenters. This, of course, is as it should be, for an institutional vision and the diversity of institutions and their unique goals, locations, histories, and constituents is a highly valued characteristic of our nation's colleges and universities. The institutional perspectives are summarized below as they were presented, and the chapter concludes with my own observations on the issues raised in the panel discussions.

## AN OVERVIEW

David Ward, the President of the American Council on Education and Chancellor Emeritus of the University of Wisconsin-Madison, was the moderator of the panel. His perspective was that transformational change would be hard to come by because there are three components of alignment: what the public thinks, what policymakers think, and what higher education leaders think. He suggested that transformational change would probably mean structural change and that there were, among many others, two areas in which change seemed critical: the cost of education and international competition.

Regarding costs, he noted the concerns on a broad front from business practices to tuition, but that the public has high anxiety about cost, not about accountability. He believes that the Spellings Commission was very creative in dealing with affordability and access. He noted that it was really concerned about international competition and raised a much broader issue of access – of leaks in the educational pipeline. The question, as he stated it, was whether the schools were preparing students that would form human capital by being effective in college, in graduate school, and in high-tech knowledge-based employment.

The pressures for accountability, according to President Ward, should not be seen as a statistical end – not 'just a mindless desire' for more data about whether colleges are doing what they say they do. Rather, the use of accountability seems to be driven by the need to know whether our colleges and universities are effective in meeting international competition.

Both cost and international competition entail relationships between higher education and government, and this is where structural issues arise. Ward believes that there has been an extremely creative partnership between government and higher education, whether independent, public, not-for-profit, or proprietary. That partnership rests on both civic and economic foundations. The civic base was the idea that an educated populace is a public good. There was a sort of quasi-entitlement that each generation would try to make sure that the next generation would be educated and able to improve itself – the idea of creating human capital, of opportunity, and of the social mobility that democracy represents. The economic base is simply that our economy is driven by innovation and advancement of knowledge.

Ward suggests that the prevalence of concerns about cost has obscured these two foundations of the partnership – that in society's pursuit of the private good even higher education's leaders may have lost the sense of the public good. He believes that, without question, the heart of the alignment must be reconstruction of the relationship between government and higher education, and the creation of a baseline for public investment in both democracy and economic stature.

He sees the most serious issues as access and affordability, but with others being raised along with them – for example, accountability, innovation, alternative learning models, and technology. The Spellings Commission, in most part, he believes, used great care in stating the problems that urge transformational change. But he also believes that the Commission's report placed too much emphasis on what higher education could do and too little on what government could do, particularly with respect to access.

## FOUR INSTITUTIONS

Of the four panelists reporting on alignment issues at their institutions, two represented independent universities with research capacities, one represented a proprietary institution, and one a public multicampus university system.

**Tufts University** was represented by its president, Lawrence S. Bacow, a lawyer and economist. President Bacow emphasized three difficulties facing alignment: competition among institutions, trends in student financial aid, and education of the workforce.

First, he noted the breadth of institutional competition. Some 4000 widely differing institutions compete for students, faculty, resources, and public visibility, and this competition has stimulated enormous innovation. Those who believe that higher education does not change do not realize the tremendous amount of innovation that takes place. But he also finds that the competition in higher education differs from that in business and industry. In other sectors, competition forces people to lower costs and improve productivity. In contrast, although higher education's leaders know how to constrain costs and raise productivity, no one is pounding the table to do it.

The reason for the lack of pressure for lower costs and greater productivity is pressure in the opposite direction. Families and students want smaller classes, more student contact with faculty, and fancier dormitories. Although not irrational, some of these demands are statistically independent of the educational outcomes that are the most important facet of any institutional vision; others entail dollars or faculty time that could otherwise be spent enhancing the vision; all result in reducing faculty productivity. Bacow sees a fundamental tension between those – higher education's leaders – who are responsibly trying to keep costs down and some segments of the marketplace to which these leaders are responsive. Critics of higher education often argue that we should run our institutions more as businesses are run. The fact is that we are doing so now: we are responding to consumer demands in a competitive marketplace. It is going to be hard to move beyond these conflicting interests.

Second, Bacow believes that access and affordability are major aspects of alignment, noting that independent institutions and many public ones devote substantial resources to trying to ensure access. Tufts, for example, is committed to need-blind admissions and student financial aid is the fastest growing item in its budget. The marketplace – the political marketplace – has been taking a different direction. In both public and independent institutions, the growth has been in *merit-based* aid, not *need-based* aid. Bacow considers it a scandal that our society is redirecting financial aid resources away from the needy to redistribute bright students among institutions, bright students who are certain to go to good schools anyway and whose families can afford to pay their way.

If political and educational leaders are serious about ensuring access, Bacow believes that one of the biggest transformational changes that they could make would be commitment, as a group, to need-based financial aid. He notes the Spellings Commission's consideration of financial aid and urges support of its recommendations.

Third, Bacow's final point was that liberal education, the traditional role of higher education in educating effective citizens, may be getting lost in concern over educating the workforce. The ultimate role of liberal education is not necessarily to prepare students for professional work, but rather to prepare them for life. When he welcomed freshmen to Tufts in 2006, he told them that it really did not matter all that much what they majored in as undergraduates. He gave them examples: the CEO of Pfizer was an English major at Tufts, and a four-star Marine general majored in psychology.

Bacow is concerned that the pressures of global economic competition to educate the next generation of workers will cause political and higher education's leaders to lose sight of the traditional mission of liberal education. There is much discussion at the national level about America's role in encouraging democracy throughout the world. Bacow urged that higher education has a role to play in helping to make democracy work here at home.

**Tulane University**, represented on the panel by its president, Scott S. Cowen, is an independent research-oriented institution. Located in New Orleans, Tulane suffered extensive damage in August 2005 during Hurricane Katrina. In December 2005, the university issued a Renewal Plan to address strategically its current and future operations in the post-Katrina era.

President Cowen opened his remarks by thanking the colleges, universities and higher education associations which came to the assistance of Tulane following the Katrina disaster. He stated that he believed that transformational change in higher education is extremely difficult, if not impossible, to achieve, particularly in large complex institutions. He stated that positive change is possible, but that higher education institutions are simply not structured for transformational change.

He expanded by posing four major structural barriers. First, the principle of shared governance in higher education is one such barrier. He strongly supports the principle, is aware of its very positive aspects, and sees it as one of the distinguishing characteristics of American colleges and universities. It is also a principle that distinguishes these institutions from most other organizations. But he is also aware of the downside. Because of the many people who share governance, solutions to difficult problems are usually watered down to the least common denominator.

Second, tenure is likewise a positive factor in higher education, but one with a downside. Tenured faculty members are a base that is there for a lifetime, and they often disagree, some for good reasons, some for bad. If they seriously disagree among themselves or with the board or administration, transformational change is probably impossible.

Third, tenured faculty may be the most organized of an institution's stakeholders, but they are not alone as an impediment to change. Alumni, students, staff, and even members of the local community are among every university's multiple stakeholders. Each stakeholder has a different goal, and each competes with the others – and with the institution – to achieve it.

Fourth, traditional processes for selection of boards and presidents are, in a sense, a self-inflicted barrier. Transformational change requires presidents and boards who themselves are entrepreneurial, bold, and courageous. And they need a particular set of skills for transforming an institution. Most higher education leaders would fail to meet these requirements simply because they were selected because they were fine scholars who moved up the administrative ladder without seriously rocking the boat. And board members seem to become conservative after they are selected; they become embedded in a status quo group-think milieu that is almost unbelievable.

Although pessimistic about the possibility of transformational change, President Cowen was optimistic about what he calls 'enlightened incrementalism' – a middle ground between the status quo at one extreme and transformational change at the other. He defines this middle ground as the cumulative effect of getting done what can be done over time. He suggests that what is generally called transformational change is, in fact, enlightened incrementalism. In support, he reports that Charles Vest, former President of MIT, had always felt guilty about being unable to articulate a vision for that institution, but, on his retirement, he was widely congratulated on his 'terrific vision for MIT'. He then realized that it was the cumulative sum of all of his incremental changes that made the vision for which he was being thanked.

President Cowen noted that higher education is now much more flexible and progressive than in the past, and much more so than the public gives it credit for. He attributes the improvements to enlightened incrementalism in response to economic, societal and technological change. He argues that people who believe that higher education is wedded to the past are simply not cognizant of the progress that has been made.

What motivates institutions to change? President Cowen sees only two possibilities: the desire within institutions to be more effective than in the past, and the impact of a crisis.

The desire of an institution's educational leaders – its president, deans, and board – to make it better is strong motivation for change. During President Cowen's first eight years at Tulane, he and his colleagues redefined selected standards in terms of academic quality and its impact – student standards, faculty standards, and research standards. They worked hard to do so, and he believes that metrics would show improvement every year. But here again, there is a downside: programs were added and expanded but not a single thing was deleted. This is an example of barriers to change, for it is very hard to delete a traditional academic program in which faculty have a vested interest.

In President Cowen's opinion, the likeliest – perhaps the only – motivation for, or time that you can get, transformational change is a crisis. After Katrina struck New Orleans and Tulane, the university had to do something to recover and survive. In passing, he said that, although many might not believe it, there are still some people, faculty, and others, who question whether Katrina was justification for change, some even suggesting that it was just a pretext.

Tulane's plan for recovery from the Katrina crisis was motivated by the need to answer three questions:

1. How can Tulane transform itself to enhance, not just maintain, academic quality over time?
2. What can Tulane do as an institution to become more civically involved than in the past, to play a major role in the recovery of New Orleans, and to draw lessons from this effort for other communities that find themselves in a crisis situation?
3. How can Tulane transform itself to attain financial stability in the aftermath of the disaster?

President Cowen believes that Tulane's recovery plan is answering these questions. The university has pursued the plan in a strategic and surgical way, and focused precisely and only on areas that have demonstrated or can demonstrate defined academic excellence. Through this restructuring, $90 million dollars was cut from the $750 million budget. Tulane will, he believes, be a stronger and better institution three years from now than it was before Katrina. Without the crisis, Tulane would have continued on the track of enlightened incrementalism, getting better year after year, but it could not have made the discontinuous improvement that is now transforming the institution.

President Cowen's final comments related to an institution's alignment with the public and policymakers. The latter, he said, must be recognized as key stakeholders. Higher education leaders must understand what is expected of their institutions and what the institutions can deliver. He offered two thoughts on the understanding required.

First, institutional leaders have to understand the difference between the suggestions that come from policymakers or from public pressure that are sustainable and those that are merely fads. Institutions would be doing some ridiculous things if their leaders could not say 'no' to many suggestions. It is hard to say 'no' to an influential stakeholder, but it has to be done. Often a suggestion will be made simply because the policymaker has not recognized the importance or sustainability of the issue. There are valuable suggestions, however, and these are the ones that are sustainable in the long term for the good of society.

Second, even where a policymaker's suggestion is genuine and sustainable, it should be tested against the institution's own goals, priorities, and strengths. If the test fails – if it is not in line with the institution's vision and capacities – it should, Cowen believes, be rejected. Why? Because accepting it will only add costs, usually without adding distinctiveness.

There are, of course, many situations – particularly in research – where universities have been influenced by political pressure or public pressure, but fortunately most of these appear to be in the best public interest. The important thing is to separate the reality of what can and should be done from what feels good for an important stakeholder.

President Cowen concluded as he began with his belief that transformational change is a very elusive concept, and that it cannot be achieved without a crisis. He wished that higher education's institutional leaders had a few more degrees of flexibility to make significant change, for he knew of none who would not like to make his or her institution more responsive and sensitive – to make it a more powerful institution for the good of society.

**Berkeley College** was represented on the panel by its president, Mildred García. The college is a 75-year-old proprietary institution that operates six campuses in New York and New Jersey. It offers bachelor's degrees, associate degrees, and, in technology, certificate programs. It also operates an online 'campus' with students in 29 states and 88 foreign countries.

President García emphasized the differences between Berkeley College and the other institutions discussed by the panel, most distinctly in her college's direct and explicit engagement with a major national issue: how do we meet the responsibility of educating the extremely diverse student body that is becoming the United States? She said that of Berkeley College's 6000 students 21 percent are African-American, 29 percent Latino-Latina, 27 percent white, 7 percent Asian, 10 percent international, and the balance multicultural. Her own background, she noted, was similar to those of many of these students and she clearly understood the power of education.

Numerous proprietary institutions serve similarly diverse student bodies and stress education for useful employment. In January 2006, a widely viewed CBS television program, *60 Minutes*, examined allegations of fraud and misrepresentation in several of these schools. The political response was immediate: the New York Department of Education proposed new regulations, and Congress held a hearing.

President García's major concern was the loss of public credibility suffered by Berkeley College, simply because of the tendency of policymakers and the public to paint all proprietary institutions with the same brush.

The 'broad brush' treatment of proprietary institutions is a problem for President García, who noted their great diversity: some are accredited, some are not, and some offer degrees and some do not. She noted Berkeley College's accreditation by the Middle States Commission on Higher Education and its authorizations to offer bachelor's and associate degrees by New York and New Jersey. She also noted that offering a bachelor's degree in New York requires 33 percent of credits to be in the Liberal Arts and that New Jersey requires 50 percent to be such credits. She is proud of Berkeley College's retention and graduation rates, and believes the traditional institutions and the proprietary ones have lessons that would benefit one another. In this regard, four of the 15 members of her own governing board are from traditional campuses, another is a community college president, and four represent the owners.

President García discussed the dimensions of excellence and her conviction that academic excellence does not depend on whether an institution is a research university, a comprehensive one, a community college, or a proprietary one. Rather, there are many dimensions to excellence, and, whatever its classification or sector, an institution can rise to excellence if it continuously looks at what it is actually doing in terms of its mission – and is living up to that mission.

Motivation for transformational change should derive from the need to regain the trust of the public and the state and federal governments. Change in this case would require bringing the best qualities of traditional education and the best of the proprietary sector together. The result would be a new model that would successfully deal with the ethnic, economic and social diversity of today's student body. President García noted that her background was in traditional education as a senior administrator at a community college, at a comprehensive state university, and at a research-intensive one. She was a member of the Berkeley College board when appointed president.

To regain the trust of policymakers, President García believes, the proprietary colleges should recognize that the state has a legitimate interest in their quality, costs, and administration. Proposed rules in New York would, among other things, regulate the transfer of ownership of schools; have procedures for determining whether to limit or revoke degree authority when regulations are violated; and require the colleges to pay for visiting examining teams. Although the last requirement is considered by some to be inequitable, President García sees it as a small price to pay for regaining lost trust.

The task of regaining credibility includes being totally open to examination by the two states in which the college operates. President García finds that reviewing teams now look closely at things that were taken for granted in the traditional institutions where she previously worked. In this regard, she asked the states not to appoint examining teams consisting entirely of examiners affiliated with proprietary colleges, and the states have agreed. She will continue to work closely with both the New York State Education Department and the New Jersey Commission on Higher Education to rebuild trust.

**The University System of Maryland** was represented on the panel by its chancellor, William E. Kirwan. The Maryland System is governed by a single board. It and Chancellor Kirwan are responsible for 13 campuses: 11 degree-granting institutions (three of which do a significant amount of research and eight of which are comprehensive campuses) and two free-standing research institutes. They are also responsible for two regional centers. The System has an enrollment of some 130 000 students.

Chancellor Kirwan does not claim that the changes made in Maryland were transformational, but does believe that significant change was successfully made. He noted that Maryland's experience may have limited applicability elsewhere – as in politics, all change is local. The two major motivations for change, he explained, were the severe state budget problems in fall 2003 – the System's budget was cut by about 12 percent – and an expected large enrollment growth based on a projected increase of about 30 percent in high school graduates over the next seven or eight years. Compounding these problems was awareness of the System's problematic image held by the public and policymakers in the state capitol – one of inefficiency and faddishness.

To respond to the problems, a work group decided to look at all System processes, academic and administrative, and to focus on maintenance of academic quality, increasing efficiency and effectiveness, and holding down growth and cost. Despite the large size of the System, the 18-month process of planning for change was very collaborative, one that engaged the board, the chancellor, the presidents, the provosts, faculty, and staff. In the early stages, the System was assisted by an outside consulting team.

There were substantial results of initiatives at the completion of the first phase of this 'effectiveness and efficiency' effort:

- The faculty teaching commitment was increased by 10 percent across the System. Each institution has different teaching expectations, and the increase was an average for the institution. How to meet the increase was left to the deans and department chairpersons.
- The standard number of 120 credits required for a degree was found to have crept up to 130–35 in many programs. The new policy required that any increase over 120 credits had to be justified by the board. Exceptions were made for accreditation requirements.
- To increase classroom capacity, the System instituted an expectation that students would earn 12 credits outside the traditional classroom – through internships, work-study, online courses, study abroad, or any credit-bearing opportunity approved by the faculty.
- The System entered a partnership with a community college in one of the state's fastest growing, wealthiest counties – one that did not have a four-year institution. The community college would offer the first two years of work, and one or more of the System's universities would complete the degree program. The programs offered would be targeted to the workforce needs of the county: nursing, teaching, information technology, and business.
- The System's effort on the administrative side concentrated on functions that could be centralized without impinging on the autonomy of its campuses, functions such as audit, construction management, and real estate development. Centralization of purchasing resulted in savings of millions of dollars, according to Chancellor Kirwan.

Over fiscal years 2005 and 2006, these efforts took about $60 million of costs out of System operations, and the savings were very consciously set against increased costs to emphasize that the effort was to hold down tuition increases.

Perhaps the most high risk element of the plan was beyond the System's control. It requested that the state pick up the additional costs of the expected high enrollment increase. The System would take 25 percent of the increase without cost to the state, but the expectation was that each year the state would pay for the students above that 25 percent. The budget request was carefully targeted at state priorities, workforce and economic development, and the quality of the institutions.

As the System went to the state with its planned efficiency commitment for 2006–08, it did so with a carefully prepared report on all of the efficiency and effectiveness efforts. The report was a deliberate attempt to help people understand the problems and the System's response. The chancellor and others visited editorial boards and appeared on television and radio talk shows. The response was very positive in the media and by the governor and legislature.

So far, the alignment process has worked. In fiscal year 2006, support for the University System increased by 6.5 percent, and the tuition increase was held at 5 percent; in fiscal year 2007, the budget increased by 15 percent and tuition not at all. The System received full funding for the enrollment growth that the System could not otherwise accommodate.

These effectiveness and efficiency efforts, Chancellor Kirwan believes, are now part of the System's institutional culture. The System is now entering into Phase 2 of the effort with the help of the National Center for Academic Transformation. This second phase will explore strategies for teaching lower division courses at reduced cost, and better learning outcomes. Each campus is now engaged in at least one course transformation project on a pilot basis.

Chancellor Kirwan was confident of the good results of the efforts. He has no doubt that quality has improved; that the capacity of all institutions has increased to serve more students; and that the System has been able to hold down tuition increases. What of the future? He did not know whether a new paradigm in relationship to the state government had been achieved. He is sure that there is now a much better sense of credibility with state government. We shall have to wait and see, he said, but there has certainly been a very positive short-term effect.

# QUESTIONS AND COMMENTS FROM THE AUDIENCE

In calling for questions, President Ward, the moderator, reminded the audience that the panel was directed at alignment across three variables:

institutional vision, policymakers, and the public interest. He noted that particular concerns usually existed for each variable – for example, institutions were concerned about quality and, in many cases, about research; state policy leaders about accountability; and the public about getting jobs.

**Liberal Arts and the Preparation for Work**

The initial questioner asked for comments on what he perceived as the greater interest of policymakers and the public in workforce development than in liberal education and preparation for citizenship. President Bacow conceded this to be a difficulty, and said that it arose mainly because people were thinking primarily about undergraduate education. He urged that educators press the importance in undergraduate work of reasoning, analytic skills, capacity to ask important questions, and communication, and also the importance of graduate education as the foundation of the next generation's scientists, engineers, technological leaders, and development of the nation's competitive capacity. Liberal arts colleges and community colleges might have different focuses.

President García agreed, saying that students came to her campuses because they and their families wanted them to get a degree and get to work, but that the task of the Berkeley College campuses was to capture their imagination, to make them aware of the importance of the liberal arts and sciences, and to make them think critically about a well-rounded education. An audience member noted that the Spellings Commission agreed with this – that a broad knowledge of science and the humanities was essential. He noted that this debate was going on in Europe, where the concern was that the usual three-year degree was not enough to ensure employment. There seemed to be general agreement that both a foundation in the liberal arts and education and training for employment were essential.

**Politics**

Chancellor Kirwan was asked how he maneuvered the turbulent waters of the then-approaching gubernatorial election, in which the challenger accused the incumbent of responsibility for tuition increases. The Chancellor commented that there seemed to be an economic downturn every decade, and that higher education's budget is inevitably reduced because it is a discretionary expenditure. Moreover, he said, it is the governing board, not the governor, that sets tuition. He looked with favor on a new legislatively created commission that is looking at sustainable funding for higher education that would avoid future such budgetary ups and downs.

**Teaching and Undergraduate Education**

One questioner had two concerns. The first was how to address what he saw as the lack of attention to the teaching function, a problem that resulted in sending students into majors for which they were not prepared. The second was how to explain this institutional lack of attention to the public, particularly to parents. President Ward commented that there would be different answers for different institutions.

President Cowen said that it was not particularly difficult in a private institution to convince both parents and faculty about the value of teaching. The people who pay very high tuition demand and expect high-quality teaching. Tulane aligns incentives to reward both excellent teaching and excellent research. Balancing these is important. If undergraduate teaching is poorly performed, it has a systemic impact on the entire university. He admitted to a problem in educating parents – their conflicting expectations: they want small class sizes and one-on-one contact with faculty, but they also want lots of extracurricular activities and Jacuzzis in the residence halls. High tuition is what pays for the whole college experience. Faculty must be continually motivated both to teach and to do research at a very high level.

President Bacow saw research and teaching as mutually supportive. Students ask questions we cannot answer, and we invite them to join in the scholarly effort to explore these. Students become research collaborators, and the results should then ultimately inform the curriculum in the educational experience of the next student generation. President Bacow was not sure that enough of these opportunities were being created, but did contrast Tufts's overlapping – competitive – schools of 30 years ago with those today. Thirty years ago the overlapping schools were Amherst, Williams, and Colby. Now they are Penn, Cornell, and Columbia. Students come to Tufts because they want to be at a research university where there are opportunities to react with faculty, not just at the college but also at the seven other schools and four affiliated teaching hospitals. Parents should be engaged in conversations that explain how the research enterprise and teaching are not competitive but reinforcing.

President García remarked that Berkeley College did not have a formal research function, but that every institution, whatever its mission, should ensure that teaching and some relevant research go hand in hand. She was aware that in some institutions faculty involved in research considered teaching students a burden, but this was not an issue at Berkeley College, where parents and students saw education and teaching as central to economic survival.

President Ward said that he thought that teaching and/or research was probably more of an issue at the large research universities than at other types of institutions. But he added that the past decade has seen substantial response to perceived conflict in the greater emphasis on undergraduate education. In part, this response is motivated by the desire to attract better students, but the whole institution is benefited by the increasing number of small learning environments within the larger institution. The examples he gave were residence halls devoted to an academic theme, and faculty offices in residence halls.

President Cowen suggested that a post-Katrina experiment at Tulane might be of interest to others. As part of the recovery process, all professional and graduate schools have been asked to participate in undergraduate education. The schools of medicine, law, social work, and public health and tropical medicine are now all involved in undergraduate education as they never were before the storm. The School of Social Work now offers two undergraduate electives, for example, and the School of Medicine, which has always opened its laboratories to bright undergraduates, is now teaching an undergraduate course on medical ethics. He does not know whether this can be sustained over time, but finds the early results very encouraging.

President Ward asked permission to comment on undergraduate work and teaching. He thought that the 1980s were probably the peak of public and parental complaint about the quality of undergraduate education at comprehensive universities, and noted that a survey at the Madison campus of the University of Wisconsin had looked at the relationship between teaching quality and research preeminence. Eight departments were high in both. In only one department was research very high and teaching quality very low. He suggested that the response will differ according to the extent of research. If research is extensive, then it is important to take steps to balance it with teaching. In contrast, if research is modest or fragmented, then the commitment to teaching should be the institution's core mission.

An audience member suggested that legislators do not care whether faculty do any research at all. At the same time, mid-level institutions want faculty to do research to stay informed and aggressive in their particular fields, but the legislators would be happy to have them teach four or five classes per semester. President Ward agreed that his own fondness for sixteenth-century Elizabethan literature could be a field in which legislators and the public might not be interested, but they certainly show strong interest in research that connects with economic development. He noted that the states, not the federal government, are investing extensively in stem cell research. President García cited the regular meetings of institutional presidents in New Jersey who are talking about the importance and impact of research in the Solutions for Our Future project.

President Ward added that the Solutions project was based on 21 focus groups across the country, and that the speaker and the questioner were correct: it was very hard for the public to verbalize what they liked about research. They understood why they liked teaching immediately, but it was not until they were given the language and concept of discovery, innovation and growth that the importance of research became clear. In passing, President Ward added that he does not think that enough has been done to promote research in the humanities; the most enduring products of our society are art, literature and music.

President Ward's final point was the contrast between the rapidity with which information and innovation about research spread within disciplines and the individualistic parochialism of information about teaching. Some of the most dramatic breakthroughs in teaching are not broadly shared and remain locked in one institution. He suggested the need for a clearinghouse where useful ideas about instruction could be widely shared.

## The Spellings Commission

An audience member was of the opinion that higher education collectively had been too critical of the Spellings Commission's report. He said that higher education had acted just like any industry subject to an unfavorable report by circling the wagons and saying that it was a bad report. A better posture, he suggested would be to have embraced the report's positive aspects – for example, the recommendation for increased funding to increase access. President Ward replied, saying that he did not think that higher education had been negative. He thought that it had walked a tightrope by saying that there were good points and that higher education should leapfrog beyond the report to take ownership of the good issues the Commission raised. He was impressed by the Commission's balanced approach, although there were some exceptions.

**Research and Teaching**

The relationship between research and teaching was a recurring topic throughout the discussion, and was well summarized in a final comment by Ralph Hexter, President of Hampshire College. President Hexter agreed with a comment of President Bacow that it is a mistake to treat research and teaching as opposites, because they are functions that go together. What is so important, he said, is the value of having research-active teachers, and there is a need for students to understand what it means to be discovering what is new, what is not yet known. Unless this is done, the nation will not be able to maintain an innovative economy. It is not only desirable but necessary for all institutions to find ways of bringing all the pieces of teaching and research together. President Ward commended President Hexter for his appropriate concluding comment.

## CONCLUDING OBSERVATIONS

The panel discussion by four college and university leaders offers a rare opportunity to look seriously at both the details and the broader aspects of institutional change. It was tempting to draw a little matrix to 'compare and contrast' the organizational types, the reasons for change, the strategies to undertake it, and the problems and opportunities it presented. The temptation was resisted, however, in part because of doubt that such an analysis would be particularly useful; in part also because of Scott Cowen's comments that 'transformational change' only occurred in response to a crisis, was 'discontinuous', and was, in any event, an 'elusive' concept. My observations are still of the compare and contrast genre, but of two concepts: transformational change, from the title of the conference, and alignment, from 'aligning' in the title of the panel.

Transformational change was not defined for the panelists, and most were in some doubt about whether the change in their institutions could be so characterized. Their doubt is warranted, for transformational changes are rare and arise from major changes in American society. None would disagree that the following are three examples of transformational change:

- *Economic factors* The Land Grant Acts were enacted as industrialization grew and agricultural practices improved; they were a major stimulus to the establishment of state colleges and universities.
- *War* The GI Bill educated an enormous number of returning veterans who would otherwise have not aspired to higher education. Federal reliance on research at universities during World War II and the Cold War resulted in today's great research institutions.
- *Demographic factors* Although not originated for that purpose, the community colleges grew in numbers of students and campuses to respond to the baby boomer generation.

The common elements suggest a definition: transformational change is institutional response to major societal change when that response requires new missions, policies or structures.

Alignment is also a response, but one that takes place within a context of relatively stable expectations and relatively stable institutional aspirations and expectations. Colleges and universities expect enrollment to fluctuate, governmental policies to shift with elections, and the economy to move up and down. Alignment addresses issues that are widely shared and responses based on past experience and the assumption of continuing institutional missions and conceptions of quality. Alignment – like government itself – is necessarily imperfect, for its goal is maintenance of a balance of institutional mission and capacity with external and uncontrollable pressures from two sources, an ever variable market and shifting state and public priorities. This 'triangle of tensions' – the institution, the market and the state[1] – is normal, and institutional leaders spend many days and hours managing it. For example, Scott Cowen notes that even the best ideas urged by policymakers must be tested in terms of their compatibility with the institution's mission and its capacity to implement them. On fortunately rare occasions, it may be necessary to exacerbate tension; the historical values of higher education should prevail, for example, when political extremists (such as Senator McCarthy) attempt to impinge on them.

Every business has at least minimal structures and processes to alert it when alignment with its environment is required: annual review of a profit and loss statement and a balance sheet by management and the board of directors. But even with the best quantitative indicators of the need for alignment, change is difficult: so difficult that procrastinating alignment may lead to the even greater challenge of transformational change – the current plight of America's 'big three' automobile companies may be a case in point. On the other hand, if transformational change were required, a business or industrial organization would have many more options for response than would a college or university. How many universities have sold or spun off a medical school?

If it is difficult for business, determining the need for alignment is even more so for higher education, where direct quantitative measures of progress are lacking. The relationship between a college's costs and its revenues is important to the administration, but says little about either the quality of instruction or the relevance of its programs to public goals. On the other hand, as Scott Cowen points out, colleges and universities have structural characteristics that facilitate alignment. Tenure, the processes of selecting presidents, and the institutional conservatism of governing board members are all factors that favor conventional responses to a wide range of expected environmental changes. Higher education often bears, disproportionately, the burden of state revenue shortfalls. In turn, colleges and universities often shift the burden to students by first raising tuition and fees and then making up the balance by across-the-board cuts to academic schools and departments. The conventional response is not always the wisest or fairest course, but it is quick and, almost by definition, the accepted one. The shared expectations that facilitate alignment are, however, a serious obstacle to transformational change, for the latter breaks continuity with the past, entailing either redefinition of an institutional mission or drastic restructuring of the means of accomplishing it.

It is much easier to distinguish between the eras of alignment and those of transformational change retroactively – historically – than it is in one's own time and at one's own institution. It is probably best to think of these as the extreme points on a spectrum or scale that reflects the extent of the impact that external factors have on the institution. At one extreme, alignment usually has relatively little impact – for example, each annual adjustment to the institution's budget, if the latter is within an expected range of possibilities. At the other extreme, transformational change can have a dramatic impact – for example, shifting the governance of a state college campus to a research university's multicampus system. Going back to the budget example, even if the budget were below the expected range, response to it would still be alignment if the reduction were attributable to a one-off event, such as an unforeseen state revenue shortfall. Institutional response would move up the scale, however, if consecutive budgets were unfavorable and had substantial impact on the institution's mission. Several years of declining enrollment, numerous faculty departures, or fewer new research grants are other signs that more extensive changes might be in order. Someone must read these signs for appropriate response to external change.

The role of higher education's leaders is critical to navigating through the issues of alignment and transformation. They must read the signs; must determine whether today's 'moment in history' is one of alignment or transformation; and must frame an appropriate response. Institutional leaders – presidents and chancellors – are in higher education's trenches, and, as this panel so clearly shows, the most effective leaders are adept at alignment, recognize a crisis when they see it, and can respond appropriately.

No one can ensure correct prediction of alignment or transformation, nor can anyone have confidence that response to a particular environmental change is appropriate. What can be done, however, is to identify and monitor developments that are relevant to the relationship between American society and higher education in the short to medium term, and to do so in the context of the probabilities of transformational change.

Some such developments are:

- the emergence of the knowledge-based global economy with its unprecedented demands for college-level education and skills, as well as for innovation;
- demographic change, particularly in the nation's young population: as baby boomers leave the workforce, they can be replaced

only by students from low-income and ethnic communities, students with which American education at all levels has been the least successful;

- financial constraints on state and federal government arising from growing entitlements, particularly from healthcare, but including opposition to tax increases;
- the spectacular improvements in educational participation and attainment by other countries, many of which are our nation's actual and prospective economic competitors;
- the use of technology for instruction, training, and information, a problematic area because of its rapid changes and its complexity for all except specialists;
- public policy pressures for increased degree and certificate completion rates and for demonstrable learning measures, raising, among others, the question: how to define educational quality at the undergraduate level – and who will do the defining?
- the national interest in higher education policy symbolized by the Spellings Commission; notwithstanding the wide dispersion of responsibility for higher education, several of the above developments appear to have led to growing understanding that there is a national interest.

This list could and should be longer, and others may have better ones. But these perceived developments, whether favorably viewed or not, raise issues of alignment and transformation.

Implicit in this wordy discussion of alignment, transformation and leadership examination is the core issue of public purpose. It is necessary, I believe, that higher education's policy leaders – all of them – cultivate a renewed sense of public purpose. They and all stakeholders in higher education must share a core conception of its public purpose. In the absence of such a conception – as David Ward suggested – the current demand for expensive and possibly intrusive accountability is a futile exercise. One cannot measure progress toward an unknown goal. This demand for accountability is the result of heightened public and political expectations and some thoughts about intellectual effectiveness and efficacy. Under these circumstances, it is not surprising that policy and higher education leaders now find themselves, however warily, struggling to define the norms and criteria for successful leadership of an invaluable national resource.

# NOTE

1. Clark, Burton R. (1983), *The Higher Education System: Academic Organizations in Cross-National Perspective*, Berkeley: University of California Press, p. 143.

# 4. Financing institutional operations: the entrepreneurial leader

## James C. Hearn

College and university leaders can never ignore their institutions' finances, but the current era clearly demands heightened attention. The continuation of prior levels of subsidization and research support from governments is becoming increasingly unlikely. Tuition increases exceeding inflation rates have raised pointed questions among policymakers as well as among students and their families. Personnel costs, especially for healthcare benefits, are rising rapidly. These and other pressures are pushing leaders in all postsecondary sectors toward exploring new approaches to maintaining and improving fiscal health. From reforming core financial technologies to securing new clients and new revenues from investments, the goal has been to think of finance in more creative and ultimately more productive ways. The symposium session on financing institutional operations featured four institutional leaders working to push their own organizations toward more entrepreneurial, fiscally rewarding stances. This chapter reviews these leaders' presentations and their ensuing interactions with the audience, then reflects on what the session suggests for leaders working to address contemporary financial challenges on their campuses.

## THE PRESENTATIONS

**Walé Adeosun**, Treasurer and Chief Investment Officer at Rensselaer Polytechnic Institute (RPI), tied his comments into his university's 'Rensselaer Plan'. This strategic plan points the institution toward achieving status as a 'world-class technological research university with global reach and global impact'. The major financing aspect to this desired transformational change, Adeosun suggested, was acting to increase and diversify the institution's revenue base, through creative financial and fundraising strategies. Adeosun focused his presentation on RPI's efforts to increase net revenues from tuition, research, endowment and gift operations.

In the domain of tuition, the institution sought to improve operational efficiencies and revenues and to emphasize the importance of student enrollment to the school's fiscal health. In support of these goals, RPI converted its old position of Dean of Enrollment into a new position of Vice President for Enrollment. Adeosun stressed that this new office has helped the institution increase and diversify its applicant pool while lowering its overall discount rate.

In parallel with initiatives relating to student enrollment, the institution aimed to diversify and double its annual research grant and contract awards. Adeosun suggested that, as a result, RPI has recently achieved 'exponential growth' in research funding, and over thirty new faculty have qualified for National Science Foundation (NSF) early career awards. Relatedly, after years of planning and developmental work, RPI successfully obtained funding for a new center for biotechnology and interdisciplinary studies. The new center supports ongoing research programs and helps to facilitate and encourage new constellations of effort.

In concert, the institution acted to improve its endowment operations: RPI hired its first chief investment officer (Adeosun himself), changed its endowment governance structure and processes, embraced a capital-preservation philosophy in investments, and made improved endowment performance a high priority.

The Rensselaer Plan also made development operations at RPI a major priority. The institution launched a historic $1.4 billion fundraising campaign. Additionally, capital campaigns have expanded, with particular reliance on mini-campaigns targeted on special projects and in-kind gifts. As a result, Adeosun argued, facilities have been upgraded toward improved spaces and improved technologies to better serve RPI's aspirational research mission. In addition to funding from the capital campaigns, building projects have relied upon traditional sources such as debt issuance, exploiting surpluses of existing resources, and developing strategic partnerships with corporations. Notably, working with IBM, RPI has established one of the world's largest supercomputing centers.

All of this activity has begun to pay dividends for the institution, according to Adeosun. For example, new academic programs have not only attracted new students but also produced new revenues, and the new facilities built through the campaigns have become central to RPI's position in highly competitive student markets. *Newsweek* and the *Kaplan College Guide* recently named Rensselaer one of the top 25 'New Ivies' and noted admissions applications are up substantially over earlier years (see http://www.msnbc.msn.com/id/14325172/).

**Carol A. Cartwright**, President Emeritus of Kent State University, focused on financial issues in the public university sector. Capturing the dramatic transitions in this setting, Cartwright noted that, in 1991, 'On my very first day in the office, I was greeted with the notice by the new Governor of massive state cutbacks in higher education funding. Welcome to Ohio. The university clearly had to become leaner, more focused, and extremely efficient.' The state cut back further in the following decade, and today Kent State resembles most public universities in that it receives only 'a small percentage of its overall funding from the state and is increasingly dependent on tuition and other sources'. With tuition also under pressure, it was on those 'other sources' that Cartwright focused her presentation.

While stressing that 'an entrepreneurial outlook is critical to survival', Cartwright acknowledged that faculty and staff are not always eager to change: 'The first and perhaps most important point . . . is that it's important for the leader to stand up and define reality.' Financial and strategic reality may well be far more troubling than most faculty and staff are willing to believe. Without a crisis, she cautions,

> It is extraordinarily difficult to get people in the organization to focus on the reality. The more data you have, and the more you can involve stakeholders, particularly in long-range planning, the better off you're going to be ultimately . . . People in the organization have to be part of planning for the solution to understand the realities that we're dealing with.

At Kent State, Cartwright and her team instituted a broad-based inclusive strategic planning process, including a 'cultural audit'. Through that audit, they learned that 'people within the organization did not understand how all the dots got connected'. In this context, and with increased regulations and intense pressure on accountability, Cartwright realized that institutionalizing pervasive entrepreneurial thinking would be difficult. For her, this was clearly a human-resources question: the senior leadership team must be engaged in the change and effective financial leadership must be in place. Noting that hiring a brilliant chief financial officer (CFO) was critical to her, and should be to every president, Cartwright argued that

> You want people on your leadership team who can really drill down, but you also want each leader on the team to see himself or herself as a partner, an officer of the university, a person who's expected to bring solutions, communication, problem solving and critical thinking, whether it's a problem that resides in their area or not.

Kent State's strong, empowered chief financial officer came to play a critical role in several major institutional challenges, Cartwright stated. One such challenge involved campus residence halls, a strategic asset because of the large market interested in campus housing. The university could not take the halls 'offline' because it needed the student living space, but it had to make the halls appropriate for the new generation of students in terms of safety, security, technology, and robust and attractive learning and social spaces. The leadership team learned that bringing the halls up to that standard was a '$400 million problem', and it would be difficult to solve using the standard tax-exempt bond approach. Kent State needed an innovative financial plan to sell to the board of regents that would also be affordable to students and ensure funding for the first five years of the plan. Working with the CFO, Lehman Brothers 'structured a swap approach to our bond issue, very different from the approach that most public institutions have historically used to finance projects. They were able to price the bonds to us at a lower cost, and they took on the upside potential of a variable-rate bond issue.' Kent State secured $165 million in capital funding for the first phase of the residence-hall renewal project. The lower guaranteed rate made the Kent State financial and business model work and solved 50 percent of the institution's residence-hall problem. The new halls were very attractive to students and are providing the university with additional revenues being used to support further improvements.

Increased program capacity has also been improving enrollments and thereby increasing revenues at Kent State, Cartwright argued. The institution realized that it was losing good students because it could not accommodate them in its most popular programs. So, leaders created a separate new pool of faculty positions for deans who could demonstrate how their proposed hires would increase undergraduate enrollment. Systematically tying new faculty hiring to emerging program and course demands has worked to raise enrollments and revenues, institutional analyses suggest.

At the same time, Kent State examined cost profiles for its various program offerings, and used these data to restructure curricula to lower costs at the margin as enrollments grew. For example, fashion design is a costly, studio-driven field, but Kent State faculty and staff developed an alternative degree specialty that is not so studio inten-sive, to serve students who want to work in the design industry but are not so focused on design skills themselves. This expansion of the major lowered per student costs while generating additional revenue.

Sometimes, programmatic change involved not lowering costs but instituting premium pricing where there was a fit with institutional resources and the market demand. Along these lines, Kent State decided to think entrepreneurially about its financial-engineering program. This is one of the very few such programs in the world, and it offers students an extraordinarily realistic trading floor to help prepare them for work in major financial positions. Cartwright stated that Kent State now charges 'a very substantial premium tuition for this very unusual program, and we don't apologize for it. We believe that we have a market position, a strength, and we ought to be able to provide premium revenue streams from premium pricing.'

Kent State's leaders also scanned environments aggressively for new opportunities to improve their financial position. Through such a scan, they identified a state law preventing them from investing uni-versity working capital in equities and alternative investments, as opposed to bonds. Institutional leaders lobbied along with others in Ohio, and were successful in changing the law. Now, Cartwright said, they are no longer losing millions of dollars annually from being hamstrung by constraints on their investment of operating funds. Indeed, their working capital as of the time of the symposium was about 75 percent invested in equities and alternative investments, allowing a return significantly superior to returns of the past.

Cartwright also suggested that Kent State worked aggressively to develop new markets fitting their institutional strengths. For example, they developed a new position, the Vice President for Regional Development, with the intent of better addressing needs in their home region, Northeast Ohio. And, under the same initiative, they partnered with Ohio University to network 14 campuses in Eastern Ohio in a project called 'Complete to Compete', facilitating degree completion among adult learners in eastern Ohio. With 450 000 adults who have some college education but no degree, the initiative's market potential was regarded as very significant.

Procedurally, Kent State selectively employed decentralized, responsibility-centered budgeting to respond to its financial challenges. To reward programs taking entrepreneurship seriously, they instituted a revenue-sharing model: when units can demonstrate that they are adding revenues that would not have been added under normal circumstances, they receive real financial rewards. Cartwright noted that the university's library and information sciences program garnered such rewards when their faculty, understanding their distinctive marketplace advantages, took their programming statewide through various technologies.

Kent State also became more attentive to turning campus-generated discoveries into economic development opportunities. The institution was the site of very early developments in liquid-crystal materials and still has major faculty expertise and research in that arena. Now, after substantial institutional investment in various forms of technology transfer and commercialization, those long-standing resources are paying off for the institution in new ways. Data in a recent Milken Institute report (Devol and Bedroussian, 2006) placed the institution second among US institutions in business start-ups per million dollars of research spending and eighth in patents filed per million dollars of research spending.

It is noteworthy that Kent State was reluctant to engage in widespread adoption of one of the more familiar approaches of the new higher-education finance. Regarding outsourcing, Cartwright noted, they have nearly eliminated the word from their vocabulary, preferring instead to form business partnerships: 'If it's aligned with our mission, we want to make sure that we have some control over it.' The university developed partnerships with outside parties for food services, bus services, and other operations, using the companies' technical expertise, their technology and their management while maintaining control. A side benefit of these partnerships has been an expansion in employment opportunities for students.

**Roy Flores**, Chancellor of Pima Community College in Arizona, provided the third presentation. He began by echoing a point made by others on the panel:

> One of the ways to make smart financial decisions is to ensure that the decision makers know something about finance – something as simple as

that. Very few have formal training in finance. Now, these are bright
people. They're highly motivated. But I think it would be a disservice for
a chancellor or a president not to take that into account and to deal with
each of them and to find ways that they can become more astute about
making financial decisions. I'm not talking about budgeting decisions.
Everyone has budgets. I'm talking about financial decisions – understanding the difference between marginal cost and average cost and elasticity, whether it's price elasticity or income elasticity . . .

The old things we used to learn in Econ 201, they're really applicable.
They really . . . can be taught. What we have created is an individual professional development plan for all of the administrators. We've created an
administrative academy that people have to attend and some of that training is obligatory. The basic curriculum is obligatory, and they do that
during working hours.

Flores emphasized that this training at the community college
helps administrative leaders to understand incentives, and at Pima,
'We're busy creating incentives.' For example, new programs at Pima
Community College are funded by a special venture-capital fund. To
obtain funding, departments have to submit a formal business plan
demonstrating that the program is going to break even in three years
or, if it is important strategically, that the losses can be acceptable.
Thus, the institution requires an advance understanding of the
expected revenues and costs. If accepted, a program gets at least a
two-year commitment under the fund.

Another incentive encourages units to seek opportunities to
provide contract training. Pima is a multicampus institution and,
when a campus identifies an opportunity for contract training, it gets
a set percentage of the tuition revenue to spend for any legal purpose,
regardless of whether that program will eventually be housed on its
own site. Flores noted that this incentive program 'motivates people
to look for opportunities for the other campuses, so the campus is
without walls, as it were'.

Along similar lines, Pima College has gone into several partnerships
with the University of Arizona. The problem of poorly prepared students across all postsecondary education led Pima into a contractual,
revenue-generating partnership with the university to deliver remedial
education on the university's campus. The partnership helps Pima
spread its faculty costs, as does a similar partnership serving K-12
education. Under another partnership, the college shares faculty
appointments with the university. Flores argued that this program not
only spreads costs but also is more effective educationally for both

institutions, as students and faculty come to understand other educational settings and technologies. Finally, Flores' team are working to place Pima Community College counselors at the university to help make the transition of Pima graduates into the four-year institution smoother and help ensure students' success there.

Flores and his leadership team initiated corporate partnerships, as well, to help the college deal with its fiscal challenges. The major private employer in Tucson is Raytheon Missile Systems, which perennially faces a shortage of engineers. Those challenges arise from two significant constraints. First, because of the company's many classified projects, its engineers have to be US citizens. Second, engineers recruited to Raytheon from New York and Boston or other places are often recruited away in turn by other high-tech firms. In response to these challenges, Raytheon, Pima Community College and the University of Arizona developed a partnership to produce homegrown engineers for the area. Under the program, Pima helps Raytheon identify talented high-school seniors, whom Raytheon hires selectively after their high-school graduation. Pima then provides two years of education, free, and the University of Arizona provides two years of education in science or engineering. Throughout the four years, the students work for Raytheon. When they graduate, Flores noted, they have great incentives to stay in town working with Raytheon, because it is their home town and because they already have several years working with the company.

In another partnership with Raytheon, Flores' college helps address the area's need for high-school mathematics teachers. Under this partnership, the community college provides teacher-preparation courses to Raytheon engineers contemplating retirement, so that when they retire they can start teaching immediately in local schools.

Another corporate partnership helps address a financial problem for the college while also serving a local need. College leaders noted years ago that their nursing program was generating $600 000 in annual revenue while costing $1.6 million. The college therefore had no incentive to expand the nursing program, despite its importance to the community. The college developed a partnership with local hospitals to train their employees and in return, the hospitals covered the costs and overhead of the nursing program. Both sides benefited, Flores suggested.

Pima also has created incentives in compensation by breaking salaries into two parts. Part of the annual salary increase is an across-the-board raise based largely on the expected increase in living costs, and the other part is supplemental and individualized, based on the employee's demonstrating activity valued by the college. Faculty might be rewarded for certain activities in professional development, and staff may be rewarded for applying their skills in the local community. In this way, a faculty member's participation in a teaching workshop or a staff member's volunteer work with a community-based organization can count toward his or her salary increase. Flores noted that the salary incentives for faculty and staff help them become more effective in their jobs, while also providing larger benefits: they are 'a great recruiting tool for the college, obviously, and it also helps the community'.

**James T. McGill**, Vice President for Finance and Administration at Johns Hopkins University, provided the fourth presentation of the session. Beginning with data on the impressive size, growth and diversity of higher education in this country, he focused initially on growth in philanthropy and on the many tax advantages enjoyed by US higher education, often taken for granted by leaders, faculty and staff, including favored access to tax-exempt capital markets, untaxed investment earnings, and favorable tax treatment for donors.

Counterpoising this array of advantages are a number of immediate threats and challenges, McGill noted, including ongoing and dramatic changes in the costs of healthcare, slowing or declining inflation-adjusted government funding, especially research funding, and constraints on prospects for institutional tuition increases. McGill also cautioned that, while philanthropy continues to grow, donors are becoming 'much, much more sophisticated in terms of how they want to direct their philanthropy and their involvement in it'.

There are also longer-term challenges ahead, McGill noted. Importantly, rich institutions are getting richer. McGill stated that the increase in the top ten university endowments over the last six years equaled in dollar magnitude the increase in the next 90 largest endowments. McGill attributed these gains in part to the fact that these large endowments are managed by sophisticated investment professionals not present in other institutions.

The rich also appear to be getting richer in technology transfer, McGill suggested, stressing that capitalizing intellectual property is paying off remarkably at a few institutions, such as Emory and Northwestern, but not so much at others. He lauded Kent State's liquid-crystal technologies, but noted that, 'in fact, the major payoffs for intellectual capital being taken into the marketplace appear to be going to those institutions that tend to be among the wealthier'. McGill's point is supported in recent reviews of returns to institutions in this arena (Hearn, 2006a).

Finally, McGill suggested, the rich are getting richer (or at least maintaining their position over others) in the omnipresent college rankings; he observed that there was no change between 1993 and 2006 in the top 25 national universities in *U.S. News and World Report*, for example, and only very minor shifting in places among those.

In contrast, McGill noted that internationally, 'the education world is flattening'; that is, wealth is accumulating in many countries, and other educational systems are becoming increasingly competitive with our own. Compounding this threat, McGill argued, are pressures on our governmental revenue sources and serious productivity problems. McGill stated that, while the larger economy has exhibited remarkable productivity gains, there has been very little change in the basic higher-education delivery model, and no powerful productivity increases in the sector. Indeed, one can argue that there has been some productivity loss in higher education over the past two decades, spurred by growing overhead costs, more governmental regulation and mandates, increases in inflation-adjusted salaries of faculty, and increases in inflation-adjusted administrative costs. McGill questioned whether this limited productivity trend is sustainable.

Focusing on research institutions, McGill argued that higher education's potential productivity gains are limited by three substantial constraints. First, it is increasingly capital intensive, engaged in an inter-institutional arms race for student amenities and for research stature that fuels increasing spending on buildings, equipment, and 'star' faculty salaries. Second, he suggested, because of its commitment to tenure for most faculty and tenure-like status for staff, its heavy investment in facilities, and its idiosyncratic business systems and processes, the higher-education enterprise is incapable of being nimble. Third, McGill argued, campus research efforts are not fully funded by their sponsors. Thus, the desire for stature and prestige via research propels the pursuit of research funding, which in turn loses money for the institution. McGill illustrated the point with an example from his own institution:

Hopkins as you know is a research-intensive institution. That's great . . . That's what we are. But we lose money on every research dollar that we bring in. We lose 10 cents to 25 cents depending upon the particular kind of calculation you want to make. It is not a way to financially reach the promised land.

Thinking about what the future might bring, McGill worried first about aggressive government action, including loss of some tax advantages, as has happened among other non-profit organizations, and caps or other restraints on tuition increases. Second, McGill expressed concern about the prospect of an end to past years' favorable performance in the capital markets, if borrowing costs rise, investment returns are depressed, and inflation rates increase. Third, McGill wondered whether the nation's supply of strong students may be lost, as international competition expands and intensifies. Finally, McGill saw little prospect for an end to rising after-inflation expenses for faculty salaries and facilities.

What to do in response? McGill recommended that institutions explore three entrepreneurial approaches. First, he advocated investing more heavily in administrative technologies; that is, institutions should consider purchasing integrated business software and resource management capabilities. These investments, while expensive and time-consuming on the front end, promise to facilitate effective business practices saving institutions significant money.

Second, McGill advocated new models for research management, focused on avoiding duplication of expensive facilities, building just-in-time, limited-life structures, and maintaining flexibility to cut costs quickly. That flexibility can be achieved, he argued, by leasing rather than buying space and equipment and by aggressive 'tenuring-down' of the faculty (that is, lowering the institution's overall percentage of tenured faculty).

Third, McGill advocated exploration of outsourcing for some administrative applications. Business officers in particular, McGill argued, are too quick to reject outsourcing, saying 'We're too special. We're too complicated. We cannot lose control.' McGill emphasized the potential payoff, however: if outsourcing reduced administrative costs by a third on a campus where administrative costs are a fourth of all costs, total institutional costs would be cut by 8 percent.

McGill concluded his presentation with a somber note stressing the limited patience of our public sponsors with cost rises:

We have an economic model that's not sustainable. We have it because we have enjoyed the forbearance of government and our publics and our philanthropists . . . The perception is that higher education is becoming a private good, that is, accruing to the individual, rather than a public good. That shift in perception, if indeed it is fact, . . . foreshadows substantial pressure on us. And so it is my belief that we really need to deal with the expense side of our business, particularly in the administrative and support infrastructure.

McGill asked whether higher education is prepared to undertake the transformation necessary to meet these external challenges.

## DISCUSSION

Following McGill's presentation, the session was opened to interactions with the audience. A number of audience members directed their comments to McGill's troubling portrayal of current realities. One questioner doubted whether faculty salaries were really too high, noting that the analysis depends on the starting point for the comparisons, and suggesting that institutions need to pay well enough to be able to recruit faculty in sufficient numbers and quality to replace the many baby-boom faculty retiring in the next decade. Another audience member doubted whether administrative costs are so excessive, given the current highly litigious and customer-oriented era. Another questioner echoed the point, suggesting that, indeed, the higher-education sector often appears quite efficient compared with the business sector.

In response to a question, Flores reminded the group that sometimes the efficiency experts themselves drive administrative costs higher. Pima Community College, he noted, gets 16 percent of its funding from the state but spends over a third of that, about 7 percent of total funding, explaining to the state what they are doing with the funding they get from the state. But Flores supported McGill's emphasis on reducing costs, suggesting that it is easier to reduce budgets at the margin than to reduce administrative costs by making the lasting, fundamental structural changes needed.

Cartwright also struck a balanced tone on the efficiency issue, noting that institutions in Ohio, like those in virtually every state, pursue laudable efficiencies through healthcare and insurance collaboratives and through joint purchasing agreements, but stressing that real and important inefficiencies lie in each institution's academic core. Cartwright stated that 'The biggest challenge in trying to implement some of the efficiencies has been dealing with an organizational culture that just wants it fixed but doesn't want to have to do it in any different way.'

The session's closing interactions focused on aggressive investment approaches. An audience member began by noting that many hedge funds are 'melting down', suggesting that aggressive investment approaches may not ultimately pay off for institutions. Of particular concern is the risk that some smaller schools may get badly burned by not being able to identify and then secure the best guidance on newer forms of investment. Panelists and participants generated several responses to this danger. Smaller institutions should build networks and partner with other institutions in endowment decisions, to allow them to access the best-performing aggressive investments; leaders need to be careful to avoid taking their institution's investments into territory that is uncomfortable for that organizational culture; and managers should always set aside some portion of endowment returns as a reserve.

## REFLECTIONS ON THE SESSION THEMES AND IMPLICATIONS

The session panelists voiced similar perspectives on several fronts. Although they clearly differed in their leadership styles, the speakers consistently exhibited reliance on data to drive and defend decisions. Whether data involved the sensitivity of students' enrollment decisions to tuition levels, the extent to which technology-transfer efforts pay off, the levels of subsidization in different state systems, the returns to accountability efforts, the risks and rewards in differing approaches to endowments, global competition for students, or levels of faculty salaries, the leaders here clearly depended on solid data and argued implicitly and explicitly that effective leadership requires effective information systems.

Speakers also were consistent in voicing concern regarding the current and emerging competitive, regulatory and fiscal climate. The speakers from four-year institutions agreed that there is a continuing 'arms race' for students and research funding, and none foresaw a coming change in this environment. Indeed, escalation seems quite possible and, as one panelist suggested, standing still may really mean falling behind. Speakers appeared to agree that the stance of the

federal government is becoming more bureaucratic and less supportive of research (in real-dollar terms), imposing new restrictions and
reporting-burdens on institutions while limiting growth in research
funding. Similarly, each of the speakers from public higher education
noted the continuing constraints on state support, often in concert
with increasing accountability demands. Although recent news has
been more positive, with many state institutions experiencing a
rebound in funding (Schmidt, 2006), panelists gave no indication of
optimism for a return to state funding levels of earlier years.

Unsurprisingly, the panelists were unanimous in arguing that active
institutional leadership matters. A portrait of an effective financial
leader emerges from the session: attentive to evidence, willing to involve
a wide range of voices and expertise, open to taking risks, attentive to
mission and cautious about jeopardizing it, accepting of partnerships
with other institutions and with governments and corporations, able to
look beyond the short term into the broad future, centered on productive community relations, ethical and responsible in protecting institutional resources (financial and other), and, of course, creative.

Inevitably for any conference session, some issues were not addressed by the panelists and some issues were mentioned but could have
occupied more attention. Notably, no doubt because of their institutional affiliations, the panelists did not much deal with issues of
concern to non-selective private institutions and comprehensive, land-
grant public research institutions. Issues on those undiscussed campuses are not entirely distinct from the issues covered in the session,
but are well worth noting. For example, an Ohio State University is
different from Kent State, Rensselaer and Johns Hopkins in important
ways, including centrality in its home state, visibility in social and educational policy matters, and, of course, the magnitude of its athletic
enterprise. Likewise, a college like Tougaloo in Mississippi (small, reli-
giously affiliated, historically enrolling mainly African-Americans) is
quite distinct from the four institutions highlighted in the session.

Interestingly, the presenters evinced some differences on the value
of 'the usual suspects' in the new financial management of higher
education. For example, outsourcing seems ubiquitous across contemporary institutions, and McGill spoke positively of it, but
Cartwright expressed some doubts. At what point should institutions
say enough is enough, and reject further reliance on outsiders to
provide non-educational services in residence halls, dining facilities,
and the like? Leaders will differ on such questions, and they merit

attention. At the risk of exaggerating, one can ask whether at some point institutions' push for new management and financial models will come to threaten what Frank Newman (2000) called the 'soul of higher education'. At the same time, what educational opportunities might be lost by devoting scarce resources to maintaining traditional, institution-offered services? The topic is worth more discussion.

The session dealt little with what is perhaps the most fundamental issue facing our postsecondary system: how to improve the odds that students arrive on campus sufficiently prepared, succeed while there, and graduate with the degree to which they aspired. Obviously, this was a session on financing, not academic success, and no one would doubt the commitment of every campus to student achievement. Still, facilitating student success in college has become a major national and state priority (Hearn, 2006b), and financing and student success are not independent concerns. Ensuring student success can be expensive. Any college could be made more efficient, at least by some definitions, by being allowed to accept only those students who are well prepared and highly motivated to succeed, thus reducing chances of drop-out and reducing expenses for recruitment, orientation, remediation, transfer operations, and so forth. Few colleges have that luxury, however, and fewer still would accept so homogenous a student body (such students would tend to come from predominantly middle and higher socioeconomic backgrounds, from the strongest secondary schools, and so forth). Given the call for US colleges to extend access and reflect the diversity of the country, the question is how we can meet the needs of students needing special academic and social support systems without breaking the bank.

Many institutions have met these challenges via systematic enrollment-management systems. Such systems help institutions target their tuition levels, admissions, and aid offers toward producing a student body that is financially rewarding and academically attractive for the institution, then help institutions maximize student success on campus, directing support services squarely on those most in need of them (Ihlanfeldt, 1980). For understandable proprietary and competitive reasons, many aspects of individual schools' enrollment-management systems remain invisible to outsiders, who can only observe as an institution's student body evolves. Thus, for some external critics, there remains the uncomfortable sense that these systems can disserve larger societal goals. A pioneer in enrollment management, Don Hossler (1984, p. 61), was among the first to identify this danger:

Enrollment management carries with it an implied emphasis on productivity, efficiency, and results. Indeed, with such an approach it might be possible to develop an enrollment plan that effectively allocates financial aid with no thought to issues of equity or access. Colleges and universities do need to be managed more effectively, but they do not exist only to sell a product. Enrollment managers must take into consideration the mission of the institution as well as concerns for a more equitable and democratic society.

Competitive conditions and financial pressures have only grown in intensity in the years since Hossler's statement.

Thus, returning to the 'rich getting richer' theme raised in the session, wealthier students can potentially benefit disproportionately in admissions and services from enrollment-management efforts. They also can benefit disproportionately from recent governmental and institutional policy trends favoring merit- over need-based financial aid (Heller, 2002; McPherson and Schapiro, 2002). Sadly, evidence may begin to accumulate suggesting that institutions' and governments' ongoing financial constraints are working to make higher-education success even more stratified than is presently the case.

It will also be unfortunate if funders lose sight of bigger goals as they push to improve higher education. For example, although declines in real state funding for higher education have slowed or reversed recently, there is no apparent parallel decline in the demands states are placing on institutions to provide quantitative evidence of their efforts, via 'performance reporting' (Burke and Minassians, 2002). Accountability regimes cost money, and it seems incumbent on states to consider those costs along with the returns to the effort. A corresponding argument could be made concerning the rising accountability demands associated with federal funding. This concern parallels concerns among leaders at the K-12 level over the high implementation, maintenance and enforcement costs associated with the federal No Child Left Behind initiative: a good cause is worth pursuing only so long as the costs are appropriate relative to the returns. Institutional finances are best directed toward improvements in educational quality, and to the extent that funds are instead directed to reporting requirements having little functional impact on quality, higher-education students and the larger society may suffer.

Panelists in the session touched briefly on questions of innovative pricing. It would be a rare public or private institution that has not yet examined the recent trends toward unbundling tuition and fees, instituting new user fees, and raising tuitions in concert with increased discounting. Pricing innovation can also extend beyond those familiar topics, however. Aggressive differentiation in course and program pricing is a noteworthy case in point. Different academic courses and programs have different cost profiles and different market niches, and they can potentially have different pricing and revenue profiles as well. Leaders whose institutions have at least some pricing discretion need to utilize data on program costs and student demand to explore whether certain new and existing programs can and should be priced differentially from others. Price differentiation can be based not only on a course's associated equipment, space and salary costs but also on such factors as enrollment numbers, the qualifications of instructors, the time of day or year of the offering, or simply the going market rate. Of course, any discussion of price differentiation involves considering the extent and nature of cross-subsidization across programs on campuses, not always an easy topic (Bok, 2003). Still, active price differentiation can bring appealing financial returns as well as risks.

Some of the presenters touched briefly on the related issue of decentralized decision-making and budgeting, that is, granting academic colleges, departments, centers and other units increased fiscal and academic autonomy in concert with increased accountability. Decentralized approaches, variously termed 'incentives-based', 'responsibility centered' and 'every tub its own bottom' approaches, are frequently cited and discussed as a critical element in the new entrepreneurial emphasis on campuses. Unfortunately, we are only now seeing substantive growth in the literature covering the virtues and risks of these approaches (Priest and St. John, 2006; Hearn et al., 2006). As Ehrenberg (2004, p. 276) has noted, if institutions are to adopt decentralized approaches, the 'designs of academic governance structures need to pay serious attention to reducing problems that decentralization will cause', including decreased attention to the common institutional good, duplication, inattention to broadened access, and inattention to cross-disciplinary possibilities. Encouraging an entrepreneurial mindset among faculty and mid-level administrators can be a good thing, but the potential costs should always be borne in mind.

Limited time in the session meant limited attention to another fiscally-driven approach emerging on campuses: more entrepreneurially focused human-resource policies. As noted briefly in the session, institutions can separate individual faculty and staff salaries into a steady, cost-of-living-based core component and a supplemental 'at risk' component. The latter forms a basis not only for high rewards for especially productive employees but also for an implicit financial sanction for less productive faculty and staff. This approach to faculty and staff salaries was pioneered in university medical schools in the 1990s, and is arguably more incentives-based and performance-sensitive than the traditional approaches to compensation in higher education (Hearn, 1999). As McGill noted in the session, institutions can also pursue 'tenuring-down' of their faculty workforce. Tenured-faculty salaries are almost always the largest financial commitments institutions face, so colleges and universities seeking greater organizational agility are reducing their tenured faculty ranks via attrition and increasing their reliance on part-time and contract faculty labor (Rhoades, 1996; Ehrenberg and Zhang, 2005). What these innovative human-resource approaches produce, both financially and academically, needs to be systematically addressed.

This session, and the TIAA-CREF Institute symposium as a whole, helped to address a too-often ignored problem: substantive knowledge about significant financial reforms tends to remain largely localized to home campuses and systems. Off-campus observers and competitors most often become aware of potentially useful innovations in non-systematic and particularized ways, frequently via unpublished reports and informal networks. This knowledgability gap is troubling for at least two reasons. First, higher education remains a public as well as a private good, notwithstanding many policymakers' current emphasis on individual returns to college attendance. Its improvement is, at least in part, a collective responsibility and provides a collective benefit. Thus, all institutions are served by widening understanding of what is being done, and what is working and not working, on other campuses. Second, from an analytic perspective, too little is understood concerning the nature and interrelations of the many fiscal innovations of recent years. It appears that many of these innovations share conceptual and strategic origins in the push to markets and entrepreneurialism, but how might innovations be categorized and how are they associated? For example, are public institutions adopting decentralized budgeting more likely to also be adopting salary bonuses and privatized tuition pricing? What does the conjunction of innovations on a campus bring, compared with the effects of innovations introduced individually? Systematically addressing these kinds of questions is central to better understanding the significant reforms observed in recent years.

Most needed in virtually any consideration of new models for action in higher education is attention to failure. What failures have institutions experienced as they act to meet financial challenges, and what can be learned from those failures? Without information on poor and unexpected outcomes, it is difficult to discern what was behind any positive outcome. Presentations and writings focused solely on 'best practices' are enormously useful, but taken alone they cannot and should not drive action. Only through exposure to a range of evidence on the benefits and costs of different innovative approaches can leaders and institutions come to appreciate what is most likely to work, and not work, in their own setting.

Obviously, individual institutions cannot do all the required research on particular financial innovations themselves, but the building of larger communities of analysts sharing outcome findings across campuses makes sense. Organizations like the Association for Institutional Research can help in this, as can smaller, more regional and sector-specific collaboratives. Whatever the means, the impulse to study and share should be encouraged. Colleges and universities are by no means the only organizations suffering from an absence of commitment to what Pfeffer and Sutton (2006) have called 'evidence-based management', but one would expect no less from our knowledge-driven, knowledge-valuing culture. However strong, no one leader, institution, conference panel or publication outlet can deliver these goods, but across leaders, campuses, conferences and publications more informed and effective answers may be found.

The symposium session on financial operations was a contribution toward that goal. The session was wide-ranging and provocative, in good part because of the accumulated experience and wisdom of its panelists. Ideally, the insights of Adeosun, Cartwright, Flores, and McGill will stimulate heightened efforts toward discerning and disseminating the key factors behind successful financial innovation on campus.

# REFERENCES

Bok, D. (2003), *Universities in the Marketplace: The Commercialization of Higher Education*, Princeton, NJ: Princeton University Press.

Burke, J.C. and H.P. Minassians (2002), *Performance Reporting: The Preferred 'No Cost' Accountability Program*, Sixth annual report, Albany, NY: Rockefeller Institute.

Devol, R. and A. Bedroussian (2006), *Mind to Market: A Global Analysis of University Biotechnology Transfer and Commercialization*, Santa Monica, CA: The Milken Institute.

Ehrenberg, R.G. (2004), 'Conclusion: looking to the future', in R.G. Ehrenberg (ed.), *Governing Academia*, Ithaca NY: Cornell University Press, pp. 276–80.

Ehrenberg, R.G. and L. Zhang (2005), 'Do tenured and tenure-track faculty matter?', *Journal of Human Resources*, **40** (3), 647–59.

Hearn, J.C. (1999), 'Pay and performance in the university: an examination of faculty salaries', *Review of Higher Education*, **22** (4), 391–410.

Hearn, J.C. (2006a), 'Enhancing institutional revenues: constraints, possibilities, and the question of values', in R. Clark (ed.), *The New Balancing Act in the Business of Higher Education*, Cheltenham, UK and Northampton, MA: Edward Elgar, pp. 27–45.

Hearn, J.C. (2006b), *Student Success: What Research Suggests for Policy and Practice*, report prepared under contract for the National Symposium on Postsecondary Student Success, National Postsecondary Education Cooperative, US Department of Education, Washington, DC, November. Available at: http://nces.ed.gov/npec/pdf/synth_Hearn.pdf.

Hearn, J.C., D.R. Lewis, L. Kallsen, J.M. Holdsworth and L.M. Jones (2006), ' "Incentives for Managed Growth": a case study of incentives-based planning and budgeting in a large public research university', *Journal of Higher Education*, **77** (2), 286–316.

Heller, D. (2002), 'State aid and student access: the changing picture', in D. Heller (ed.), *Conditions of Access: Higher Education for Lower Income Students*, Westport, CT: ACE/Praeger, pp. 59–72.

Hossler, D. (1984), *Enrollment Management: An Integrated Approach*, New York: College Entrance Examination Board.

Ihlanfeldt, W. (1980), *Achieving Optimal Enrollments and Tuition Revenues*, San Francisco: Jossey-Bass.

McPherson, M.S. and M.O. Schapiro (2002), 'Changing patterns in institutional aid: impact on access and education policy', in D. Heller (ed.), *Conditions of Access: Higher Education for Lower Income Students*, Westport, CT: ACE/Praeger, pp. 73–94.

Newman, F. (2000), 'Saving higher education's soul', *Change* (Sep/Oct), 16–23.

Pfeffer, J. and R.I. Sutton (2006), *Hard Facts, Dangerous Half-truths and Total Nonsense: Profiting from Evidence-based Management*, Cambridge, MA: Harvard Business School Press.

Priest, D. and E.J. St John (eds) (2006), *Privatization and Public Universities*, Bloomington, IN: Indiana University Press.

Rhoades, G. (1996), 'Reorganizing the workforce for flexibility: part-time professional labor', *Journal of Higher Education*, **67** (6), 626–59.

Schmidt, P. (2006), 'State funds for colleges continue to rebound', *Chronicle of Higher Education*, **53** (15 December), 17.

# 5. Changing student access through strategic pricing initiatives

## Donald E. Heller

The topic of institutional tuition pricing and financial aid policies has received much attention from college and university leaders, policymakers, researchers, and the public in recent years. As the cost of college has skyrocketed, relative to either consumer prices or increases in income in the country, more and more attention is being paid to the affordability of and access to higher education. Data from the annual *Trends in College Pricing* report from the College Board (2006a) indicate that in the 25-year period from 1981 to 2006 real tuition prices (after taking into account inflation) increased 150 percent at private four-year institutions and almost 200 percent at public four-year colleges and universities. During this same period, the median income of all households in the nation grew less than 20 percent in real dollars (US Census Bureau, 2007b).

The College Board (2006b) reports that financial aid also has increased, and, in fact, the total amount of aid available has increased faster than have tuition prices – approximately fourfold during this same period. However, there have been significant changes in the type of aid that is available and who receives that aid. First, loans have become a much more important part of the financial aid landscape. While grants, and in particular federal grants, used to predominate, today federally guaranteed and private student loans are the primary source of aid, comprising over 55 percent of all aid available in 2005. Secondly, institutional grants – funded by colleges and universities either from donative funds or recycled tuition revenue – have become an increasingly important source of aid for students. Between 1992 and 2003, the volume of federal grants to undergraduates across the nation increased 96 percent, from $7.0 billion to $13.7 billion. During the same period, institutional grants increased 147 percent, from $5.7 billion to $14.1 billion, now exceeding the amount available from the federal government.[1]

The third major trend in financial aid is the increasing use of merit criteria in addition to, or rather than, financial need criteria in the awarding of aid. Historically, financial aid awarded from public funds by the federal government and states was intended largely for the purpose of equalizing postsecondary educational opportunity. The opening section of Title IV of the Higher Education Act of 1965, which authorizes the student financial assistance programs, states

> It is the purpose of this part to provide, through institutions of higher education, educational opportunity grants to assist in making available the benefits of higher education to qualified high school graduates of exceptional financial need, *who for lack of financial means of their own or of their families would be unable to obtain such benefits without such aid.* (Higher Education Act of 1965 (1965), § 401(a), emphasis added)

As stated there, the educational opportunity grants – later renamed Pell Grants in honor of Rhode Island Senator Claiborne Pell, a long-time champion of the federal aid programs – were created in order to help students with financial need to attend college. Many of the state grant programs that were developed after the passage of the Higher Education Act adopted similar need-based criteria for the awarding of their grants.

While the federal government has maintained its commitment to financial need as the criterion for awarding Pell Grants, many states have begun to adopt merit criteria – such as standardized test scores or high school grades – for awarding their grants to undergraduate students. In 1993, grants awarded by the states without consideration of financial need totaled approximately $240 million, or less than 10 percent of the total aid awarded by the states that year. By 2003, this amount had increased to $1.6 billion, or over 25 percent of the total (Heller, 2006).

Institutions have awarded both need and merit grants since the colonial era.[2] As in the states, however, merit aid awarded by institutions has been growing more rapidly than need-based grants. In 1995, higher education institutions awarded a total of $6.9 billion in grants to undergraduates, with 35 percent of this total awarded without consideration of the financial need of the student or her family. As noted earlier, by 2003 this amount had increased to $14.1 billion, with over half – 54 percent – awarded on the basis of merit criteria, rather than need. In contrast to institutional need-based grants, which are targeted at students from lower-income groups, merit grants are awarded disproportionately to students from higher-income families (Heller, 2006).

Issues of access and affordability can be approached from a number of perspectives. Individual colleges and universities are generally concerned with institutional finance, particularly those institutions that are very dependent upon tuition revenue in order to balance their budget each year. An inability to meet enrollment targets for an entering class of first-year students – or persistence rates for continuing students – can result in a shortfall of revenue that can threaten the financial health of the institution.

But higher education institutions are concerned not only with the total number of students they enroll but also with *who* enrolls. The racial, ethnic, and socioeconomic characteristics of the student body are important considerations for many institutions which strive to enroll a group of students who are at least in part reflective of the diversity of the American people. Tuition pricing and financial aid policies can be used to influence both the number of students enrolled and who enrolls. The increasing use of what has been termed 'enrollment management', 'tuition discounting', or 'strategic pricing' techniques – by both public and private colleges and universities – has been well documented.[3]

Some observers have criticized the practice, linking its increasing use to restrictions on access to higher education by lower-income and minority youth. Others have praised it as necessary for survival for many institutions, particularly those that are less selective in admissions and therefore have less market power to attract students.

The closing session of the TIAA-CREF Institute annual National Higher Education Leadership Conference focused on how strategic pricing policies by colleges and universities can impact access to higher education. The panelists in this session were James Garland, President Emeritus, Miami University of Ohio; James Scannell, President, Scannell & Kurz, Inc.; Catharine Bond Hill, President and Professor of Economics, Vassar College; and Robert G. Templin Jr, President of Northern Virginia Community College. The session was moderated by Ronald G. Ehrenberg, Irving M. Ives Professor of Industrial and Labor Relations and Economics, Cornell University, and Director of the Cornell Higher Education Research Institute.

The speakers in this session brought a wide range of experiences with these issues. James Garland was the President of Miami University when it implemented an innovative pricing structure for a public university, one that has been examined by many but has yet to catch on with other institutions around the country. James Scannell is the president of a consulting firm that is very prominent in the business of helping colleges and universities to implement strategic pricing strategies to help them achieve specific financial and enrollment goals. Catharine Bond Hill, who took office as President of Vassar College in 2006, is an economist who has conducted research on tuition and financial aid policies at selective institutions. And Robert Templin Jr is the president of the country's second-largest community college, in Virginia, a state that has recently implemented an innovative tuition pricing policy for students who transfer from community colleges to four-year institutions.

# PRESENTATIONS

## James Garland

James Garland opened the session by setting the context for the changes that he helped to implement at Miami University. He described the constraints on state appropriations facing many public colleges and universities across the nation, and the impact this has had on these institutions. A few of the examples he provided were:

- Florida's 11-campus university system is considering a 7 percent tuition increase next year, or about twice the rate of inflation. The Chancellor of the Florida System, Mark Rosenberg, was quoted as noting, however, 'That won't even put a dent in the university system's needs' (Colavecchio-Van Sickler, 2006).
- The *Los Angeles Times* reported about the deteriorating state of the physical plant at the University of California at Berkeley, described by Garland as 'the nation's highest-ranked public university': 'The campus has nearly $600 million in deferred maintenance costs and struggles to keep roofs patched, pipes sound and heating and ventilation systems working. It no longer washes windows, waxes floors, replaces worn carpets or paints interior walls' (La Ganga, 2006).

- Ohio's 13 public universities have a backlog of $5 billion of deferred maintenance, or as Garland noted, 'roughly ten times the biannual capital appropriation in the state to higher education'.

Garland went on to note another symptom of the constraint on state appropriations. The salaries of professors at public universities, which half a century ago were higher than at private universities, now lag behind by an average of $30 000. He also described another cost-cutting move, noting that at public institutions 'More than half of credit hours are taught by temporary non-tenure track instructors.'

But perhaps the biggest impact Garland discussed concerned the rising tuition rates charged by public colleges and universities and the effect this has had on some students: 'For half of the American public that financial burden is an affordable burden if families do careful planning. But for the bottom half of the socioeconomic strata in this country, it is simply an unaffordable burden.'

Garland discarded the notion that the problem of state support for higher education can be solved simply by college presidents pleading for more money from state legislatures and governors. He points instead to 'fundamental social and economic forces that have simply undermined the historic business plan of public higher education'. These forces include an aging populace, increasing costs for health-care and social programs, and increasing demands for funding for prisons and K-12 education – all factors that are likely only to increase their demands on state budgets in the future, he noted. And as these other areas take a larger and larger share of state resources, higher education is scheduled to receive proportionally a smaller and smaller share, thus putting even more pressure on public institutions to raise tuition prices.

In order to try to address these problems, Garland described how Miami University instituted an innovative tuition model in 2003. Miami eliminated the subsidized tuition price for Ohio students, and raised the rate they paid to the higher rate paid by students from outside the state. Simultaneously, however, the university provided a base scholarship to all Ohio residents (though the amount of this scholarship was less than the increase in the tuition price), with some students receiving more than the standard amount according to their financial need and/or according to merit. Thus, some students – those receiving just the base scholarship – paid more than under the old model, some paid about the same, and some students actually paid less than they would have before the policy change.

At the time Miami University announced the new policy, some questioned what impact it would have on access by lower-income Ohioans (Breneman, 2003; *Dayton Daily News*, 2003). But Garland noted the policy actually helped *increase* the diversity of the student body: 'The very first year, we saw a 40 percent increase in first generation college students enrolling at Miami University, more than a 20 percent increase in our minority enrollments, a significant increase in the socioeconomic diversity of our entering class. And these numbers have held up since then.'

Garland used the Miami experience as a model for turning other public universities into what he described as 'tax-exempt corporations analogous to private colleges'. He was careful to state that he was not arguing for privatizing public institutions; rather, he noted that the assets and title to the colleges would still be held by the state. But instead of the broad subsidy currently provided by most states to public institutions, he said, the money should be provided directly to students in the form of scholarships, targeted primarily at low- and middle-income students, which could then be used at any public *or* private institution in the state. Such a move, he claimed, would 'allocate state dollars more effectively and also provide incentives for colleges to operate more efficiently'.

Garland outlined a three-step plan to manage this transition, using the state of Ohio as an example. The first step would be to create a non-profit corporation for each of the state's 13 public universities. Each would be headed by an independent board, but would be required to honor 'existing personnel and pension obligations, research, grants, and other legal commitments'. He noted that not all parts of each university need be turned over to the non-profit corporation; he cited agricultural and education schools as those that perhaps would remain under state control, as well as branch campuses of the universities and the state's community colleges.

After this legal change was implemented, the second step would be to phase out the general subsidy each institution received from the state. He suggested a six-year period for this transition, as this is the timeframe in which most students graduate from the universities. The majority of students who entered each institution when it was still supported through public funds would thus not be unduly penalized by an immediate withdrawal of that support.

In parallel with the phased-in reduction of the state subsidy, the third step would entail a shifting of these funds to scholarships for state residents. Garland noted that the roughly $1 billion that the state of Ohio is currently investing in these 13 universities is equivalent to approximately $3500 per student. He proposed that the scholarships be awarded to approximately half of the students attending the institutions, suggesting that most of the scholarship money should be targeted on students from lower- and middle-income families. The state may choose to focus some of the scholarships on meeting particular needs, such as students majoring in STEM (science, technology, engineering, and mathematics) fields or others in which the state has large workforce demands.

Because only half of the students would be awarded scholarships, each scholarship would be worth about $7000, and Garland noted that the public universities would have to raise their tuition rates by an average of about $3500 to make up for the loss of the state subsidy. Assuming that the revenue tradeoff to the institutions between the lost state subsidy and new scholarship dollars is a zero-sum game, then a student receiving a full scholarship would see his or her annual costs decrease by $3500 per year while students not receiving the scholarships – largely those from upper-income families – would see an increase of $3500 per year, or about 20 percent of their current costs. Garland argued that because these students have 'significantly lower price sensitivity than the middle- and lower-income groups, the added cost would not be a significant barrier to their getting a college education'.

A key characteristic of these scholarships is that they could be used at any public *or* private institution in the state. This feature, Garland noted, is what would help drive the public institutions to be more efficient and more responsive to the demands of the market. As he noted,

> The 13 public universities would do everything possible to recruit these students to make up their loss as a public subsidy. But students would choose those colleges that offered them the highest quality programs, the right curricular options for them and the most value at a competitive price. Schools that found themselves losing their market share would have to improve or risk going out of business.

As to the argument that increasing the net price paid by higher-income students – and thus decreasing the gap in prices between the public and private sectors in the state – would drive more of the upper-income students to private institutions, Garland noted that after they implemented their new pricing policy at Miami University, applications from the upper-income students actually *increased*, a phenomenon he noted he was 'still trying to understand'. What Miami may have witnessed is something that economist and former college president David Breneman has labeled the 'Chivas Regal' effect (Breneman, 1994). This is the notion that students (and their families) equate the price of a college with its perceived quality; that is, that more expensive institutions are perceived to be better simply by virtue of their higher price, even in the absence of confirming evidence.

Garland argued that his proposal was an improvement on the broad, universal type of subsidy that almost every state still uses for funding public higher education institutions. The problem with this historic model, he noted, is that 'Subsidies tend to buffer organizations from competition and they weaken market-driven incentives for improvement.' He said that 'schools that found themselves losing their market share would have to improve or risk going out of business'.

Garland's proposal differs from other uses of student vouchers in one important respect: the use of financial need criteria in the awarding of the vouchers. Colorado, for example, in 2005, removed the state appropriation subsidy to public higher education institutions and replaced it with a series of College Opportunity Fund scholarships for all high school graduates in the state, as well as a series of negotiated performance contracts for services between the state and the institutions. All students in that state, regardless of financial need, are awarded the vouchers. But some observers have noted that the change in Colorado has had little impact on either institutions or students, with one noting that, 'rather than getting anything extra, students have merely become conduits for some of the money the state used to send straight to its community college system and its public four-year colleges and universities' (Thomson, 2007, p. 3).

But, in practice, one must question whether a state would allow a public college or university to actually close under Garland's scenario. Public institutions often have very powerful constituencies in legislatures, as well as among the public and local communities. The threatened closure of a college that had only recently enrolled thousands of students and employed hundreds if not thousands of individuals is likely to muster a concerted effort to save it. His proposal of a tax-exempt corporate structure for the colleges and universities could help provide some lobbying power for the institutions. So while the application of a 'market-driven' approach to institutional improvement may sound good, in practice it may be very difficult to get wide agreement to implement such a system to the point that individual institutions would be threatened with closure. Nonetheless, Garland's main point – that the long-term decline in funding for higher education as a state priority is likely to continue – remains, and his call for a new model for governing and funding public institutions of higher education bears attention.

### Catharine Hill

Before being named President of Vassar College in 2006, Catharine Hill had been Provost and Professor of Economics at Williams College. She is somewhat unusual among college presidents in that in her prior role as an economist she had conducted research on college students and the economics of higher education.[4]

Hill and her former colleagues at Williams, Gordon Winston and Stephanie Boyd, conducted a series of studies of access to selective colleges and universities by low-income students (Hill et al., 2005; Hill and Winston, 2006a; Hill and Winston, 2006b). Williams is an institution that practices need-blind admissions – admissions decisions are made without consideration of the financial need of the student – and commits to meet the full financial need of students through financial aid. Hill noted that while many assumed these policies helped poorer students to attend Williams, the institution had not looked at what low-income students were actually paying to attend. So she and Winston set out to examine the issue, first for Williams and then for a broader set of institutions (with Boyd). They used data obtained from Williams, as well as from 27 other Consortium on Financing Higher Education (COFHE) institutions – a group of highly selective private colleges and universities – to determine how much schools were actually asking students to pay for their education. They also used data from the College Board and ACT, Inc., on the income distribution of students by SAT and ACT test scores nationally.

Hill began her presentation by providing data on the net prices paid by Williams students receiving financial aid in five income quintiles. She defined 'net price' as the sticker price paid by the student – which includes tuition, fees, room, and board – less all grants received from federal, state, Williams, and other sources. What their study found was that net prices increased with income as students from higher-income families paid a higher net price. Looking at 13 years of data, ending in the 2001–02 academic year, they found that students from the bottom income quintile paid an average of just over 20 percent of the sticker price after subtracting grants. In contrast, those students in the highest income quintile receiving financial aid paid a net price that was approximately 70 percent of the total price. Hill also presented data for the 2001–02 academic year alone, which showed that the progressivity in this year was even greater than the 13-year average. That year, the students in the lowest income quintile paid less than 5 percent of the sticker price while the highest group paid about 65 percent.

Hill noted that many students from the top income quintile received financial aid and therefore did not pay the full sticker price. She reminded the audience, however, that even the students from the top income quintile who did pay full price still received a large subsidy toward the *cost* of their education. Most higher education institutions charge a sticker price less than the actual cost of providing the education, the difference being made up through donor funds and earnings on endowments, as well as through the state appropriation for public institutions.[5]

The second measure that Hill, Winston and Boyd examined was the net prices students paid as a share of the median income for each income quintile. In this analysis they found a very different picture with respect to progressivity. Even though the poorest students were paying a much smaller share of the sticker price, this still represented a much greater share of their family income. For example, students in the lowest income quintile paid a net price that was approximately 55 percent of the median income of that quintile during the 13 years ending in 2001–02. The proportion of median income paid by each group declined, to the point that students in the highest income group paid only 20 percent of median family income for that quintile.

Hill noted, however, that financial aid policy changes that were put into place prior to the 2001–02 academic year had a large impact on this measure for lower-income students. In contrast to the 13-year average of a net price that was over 55 percent of median income for students in the lowest income quintile, in 2001–02 these students paid just over 10 percent of median income to attend Williams. The highest-income students still paid 20 percent of income to attend. Thus, Hill concluded, they were doing a much better job promoting accessibility for the poorer students.

Hill then described how she, Winston and Boyd used the data obtained from 28 COFHE schools to conduct a similar analysis; the net prices for the 28 schools were very similar to those for Williams. They were interested in the question of whether the wealth of the school was related to the grant aid students from different income groups received, with wealthier schools offering lower net prices to low-income students. They did find a relationship, but, as Hill noted, 'We don't know whether it was a causal relationship', with wealthy schools being able to offer lower net prices because of their wealth. When they examined the distribution of students by income, what they found was that among these schools

> It wasn't only that they could afford to do it because they were wealthy, they could afford to do it because they weren't getting very many low-income students. So if you have a low net price for low-income students but no [or few] low-income students, that policy actually doesn't cost you very much.

Hill, Winston and Boyd's observations are consistent with the recent research of others on the dearth of low-income students at selective colleges and universities.[6]

This observation led them to look more closely at the distribution of students in the COFHE institutions. Using data from the 2001–02 academic year, they again divided the students across all 28 institutions into income quintiles. They found that only 5 percent of the students were from the lowest quintile, and only 10 percent were from the bottom 40 percent of the income distribution (family incomes below $41 000). In contrast, 70 percent of the students came from the highest income group, those with incomes above $91 700. They divided the institutions into four categories – women's colleges, coeducational colleges, Ivy League universities, and non-Ivy League universities – to see whether there were differences among these sectors. But they found a large degree of consistency, with the proportion of students coming from the top 20 percent of the income distribution ranging from 64 percent at the women's colleges to 72 percent at the Ivy League universities.

As Hill noted, this distribution may not surprise many observers who would say something like, 'By the time some low-income students get through inadequate elementary schools and even worse high schools, and who may have parents who can't or don't have the time to read to them, etc., they're not able to go on. They can't qualify to get into these schools.' In order to determine whether this assumption is correct – that poor students cannot qualify for admission to these institutions – she and Winston used the score data from the College Board and ACT, Inc., to examine how students in different income groups performed on these tests. When taking the tests students report their family's income, so Hill and Winston used the data to create a matrix of test scores (converting ACT scores to SAT-equivalent scores) by family income. The data were then used to compare the income distribution of students *by test score* nationally with that of students in the COFHE schools.

When they looked at students with very high SAT scores, Hill and Winston found that the distribution of students at the 28 COFHE schools was more skewed toward high income students than was the pool of all students nationally. For example, Figure 5.1 shows for all students scoring 1520 or higher on the SAT (or ACT equivalent score) – a very high score – the distribution of students by income quintile among the population of test takers nationally. The distribution of all students at the COFHE schools is also included.[7] At the COFHE schools, 70 percent of the students came from families with

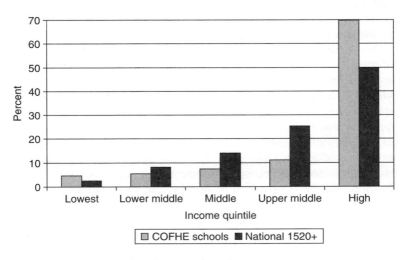

*Figure 5.1   Income distribution of students*

incomes in the top quintile, or above \$91 700. Among all test takers nationally achieving 1520 or higher on the SAT, however, only 50 percent came from this income group.

Clearly not all students attending the COFHE institutions have such high test scores, so Hill and Winston looked at the distribution of students with a lower score floor. For students with SAT scores of 1300 or above, only 39 percent of students nationally came from the top income quintile, in contrast to the COFHE institutions which enrolled 70 percent of students from that quintile.[8] At the other end of the income distribution, 16 percent of students nationally with SATs of 1300 or above came from the bottom 40 percent of the income distribution, while only 10 percent of COFHE students were from these bottom two quintiles. As Hill noted during the presentation, 'talented low-income students are out there and appear to be underrepresented at these institutions'.

In concluding her remarks, Hill noted that there are still a number of unanswered questions regarding the ability of selective private institutions to enroll lower-income students, even in the face of evidence that, as she put it, 'they're out there'. She speculated about some of the possible explanations for why these students are still underrepresented. One possible answer may be that even though many of the COFHE institutions have made strides in trying to increase the generosity of their financial aid policies, there may still be some schools that are unable to provide enough institutional grants to encourage the students from poorer families to enroll.

Another explanation she pointed to is that the admissions processes of the schools may somehow work against the needs and interests of lower-income students. She described the work of William Bowen, Martin Kurzweil and Eugene Tobin, authors of *Equity and Excellence in American Higher Education*, who have suggested that students from lower-income families deserve some form of preference in admission to elite institutions, just as athletes, legacies (children, grandchildren or siblings of alumni), and racial minority students receive assistance. Hill also pointed to potential problems with the information about financial aid that is (or is not) provided to these students. As she described it, 'We hear stories of admissions counselors in big high schools serving large numbers of low-income students saying to students, "You know, you can't possibly go there. Their tuition is over \$40 000; how are you possibly going to do that?"' She said that these institutions need to get the word out there about the availability of institutional aid and the true net prices paid by lower-income students. The final possible explanation she pointed to was that it may be a matter of the preferences of these students. Lower-income students may look at these selective colleges and universities and just not be able to picture themselves attending them and being successful once there.

**James Scannell**

James Scannell is President of Scannell & Kurz, Inc., an enrollment management consulting firm. His firm describes its services as 'developing customized financial aid/net tuition revenue and enrollment management strategies for higher education clients' (Scannell & Kurz, Inc., 2007). Prior to co-founding the firm a decade ago, Scannell served in admissions, financial aid, and enrollment management positions at Boston College, Cornell University, and the University of Rochester.

Scannell opened his presentation by describing the type of institutions on which he would be focusing his remarks, those that 'struggle every year to make their class and to be able to maybe have a couple of percent [of revenues] left over to increase faculty salaries'. These institutions, he noted, are very tuition dependent, so the implications of not meeting their targets for the size of each freshman class are quite large. He said that historically, financial aid and admissions policies had been built by institutions based on their missions – which often meant serving certain types or populations of students – along with the level of philanthropic support the institution enjoyed.

He pointed to about 25 years ago, however, as the turning point when competition, market considerations, and demographics began to shift how colleges and universities approach their use of financial aid and enrollment management. The challenge for tuition-dependent institutions in the competitive environment in which they are forced to operate today is balancing equity (in terms of the type of students who enroll) with economic efficiency. He described this tradeoff by asking the questions:

1.  will the efficient use of financial aid based on the price sensitivity of an institution's admitted applicant pool reduce access for low-income students? or
2.  can targeting aid to higher-income students to increase their probability of enrollment generate additional net tuition revenue to fund an institution's equity agenda?

Scannell said that many institutions try to achieve the second goal of enrolling enough higher-income students – who presumably do not need as much financial aid – to generate the revenue needed to fund the financial aid for poorer students, but they go about it in an ineffective manner. They often resort to tactics such as matching the merit scholarship programs offered by competitors, or relying on anecdotal evidence, or even intuition, in crafting their own financial aid programs and offers to students. He suggested that, instead of relying on these techniques, institutions should adopt a data-driven analysis: 'The problem is that we haven't used data to drive our decision making, but rather we've established a set of financial aid policies that look more knee-jerk than anything empirical based on evidence.'

Scannell acknowledged that enrollment management strategies that rely on merit scholarships have contributed to the debate about merit versus need criteria in awarding financial aid. But he noted that at private institutions especially, because of their higher sticker prices, many of the students receiving merit scholarships – those awarded without explicit consideration of the financial need of the student and his or her family – probably also have financial need. Or, as he put it, 'It's not that every merit dollar goes to those that don't need any aid at all.'

In order to demonstrate that enrollment management through strategic use of financial aid can help an institution achieve both equity and efficiency goals, he presented the case study of one institution. He described the anonymous institution as one that is located in the bottom of the first tier in its region in college ranking guides, has a small endowment, and enrolls a student body that is very diverse socioeconomically, with 94 percent of the students having financial need. The college 'hit a wall' in 2005, when both applications and the enrollment of new students declined, and net tuition revenue (tuition minus institutional grants) was flat even though the sticker price had been increased 8 percent. The enrollment of 46 students fewer than the institution's goal that year led to a budget deficit of half a million dollars, a serious condition for this school. Scannell described the college's financial aid programs as a 'patchwork quilt of guaranteed merit, affiliation awards, and partnership awards', in addition to more traditional need-based grants. Many of the affiliation awards were based on the college's mission as a Catholic institution.

Working with data from the college's admissions and financial aid files, Scannell & Kurz conducted an econometric analysis to evaluate the effectiveness of the existing aid programs. The recommendation that developed from the analysis regarding the existing programs was that the college should eliminate all of the affiliation scholarships and discounts, but continue the partnership awards and discounts offered to siblings of students already enrolled in the institution.

In addition, the institution launched 'an aggressive merit program that guaranteed an exact dollar amount of grant aid for students with specific quality levels' as measured by SAT scores and high school grades. Students could qualify for either the merit awards, or the partnership or sibling discount awards, but not both.

The result of these changes was that in the next year, 2006, enrollment exceeded projections. The institution's discount rate (total institutional grant aid divided by total tuition revenue) decreased from 36 percent to 31 percent. For transfer students, enrollment projections were also exceeded and the discount rate was reduced from 23 percent to 12 percent. The additional revenue generated by the higher enrollments and the reduction in the discount rate totaled $1.4 million if the annual tuition increase is included, and $1 million if the tuition increase is not included.

What perhaps was most important, Scannell noted, is that in implementing these changes they were able to increase their enrollment of the neediest students. The proportion of the college's students eligible for a federal Pell Grant, which is often used as an indicator of the enrollment of lower-income students, increased from 25 percent to 33 percent of the student body. He noted that while they were able to increase both enrollment and revenue, 'they didn't do it at the expense of low-income students. It wasn't an either/or, mutually exclusive proposition.'

Scannell concluded his remarks by noting that 'Using financial aid strategically, be it merit-, need-, or performance-based, to meet mission and serve students is not only ethically okay, but an absolute requirement of good stewardship.'

### Robert Templin

Robert Templin is President of Northern Virginia Community College (commonly known as NOVA), located just over the Potomac River from Washington, DC, and one of 23 community colleges in the state.

His college is not only the largest higher education institution in the Commonwealth of Virginia but also the second-largest community college in the nation (behind Miami-Dade Community College in Florida). It has over 60 000 students who are taking courses for credit, representing approximately 25 000 full-time equivalent students.

Templin opened his remarks by providing some context for the audience regarding the demographics his institution faces. Already with six campuses, NOVA is planning to build two additional campuses in the next decade, owing to surging population in the region it serves as well as increasing demand for its courses and programs. And that population is among the most diverse in the nation, with NOVA students 'representing more than 150 different nationalities', he noted. Tuition for in-state, full-time students is relatively low at just $2460 per year.[9]

The demographic demands on NOVA are fueled by the tremendous growth in the region. Templin said that, 'Of the three fastest growing communities in the United States, two of them are located in the Washington metropolitan area.' He noted that over half of the growth is from immigration, and that nearly a quarter of the area's residents are now immigrants who have arrived since the mid-1990s. And Templin noted that this immigration is not dominated by just one country or region of the world; the top four countries sending people to his region are El Salvador, Korea, Vietnam, and India. While 11 percent of the population of the United States are immigrants, in Northern Virginia the proportion exceeds 20 percent. The State Council of Higher Education for Virginia, the state's coordinating agency, projects that by 2012 the pool of high school graduates in the state will be over 50 000 students greater than in 2004, and most of these students will be looking to enroll in some form of postsecondary education.

Templin underscored the impact of these demographic changes for his institution and the state. The immigrants coming into the area are largely low-income, so tuition is likely to be a barrier for many of them, pushing them toward enrolling in community colleges rather than four-year institutions. In addition, there are no major plans for increasing capacity at the four-year colleges and universities, thus making it harder and harder for students to get admitted even if they have the resources to pay tuition in that sector.

In order to address these issues, the state proposed a Community College Transfer Scholarship. Under the original proposal, the

Scholarship will be available to students who meet the following criteria:

- They graduate from a Virginia community college with an associate's degree and a grade point average of at least 3.0.
- They have a family income of less than 150 percent of the median in the state.
- They are admitted to and transfer to a four-year public college or university in the state.

Templin emphasized that, while it is a need-based scholarship program, it is clearly not restricted to low-income students. Median family income in Virginia in 2005 was $65 174, meaning that students from families with incomes up to $97 761 could qualify for the scholarship (US Census Bureau, 2007a). Students who meet these criteria will be eligible to pay community college tuition rates at the four-year institutions, and can do so for up to 70 credit hours within a three-year period.

The state hoped that this new program would encourage more students to begin their baccalaureate education at community colleges, which have not just lower tuition rates but also lower subsidies (on a per student basis) from the state appropriation. The money the state saves by having fewer students at the lower division level of universities, and enrolling them in the community colleges instead, would be given to the four-year institutions to make up for the loss of tuition revenue from the transfer students.

Another advantage of this plan, Templin remarked, is that by having more students with bachelor's degree aspirations starting in the community colleges, it will provide them with the opportunity to prove themselves academically in a manner that they could not if they attempted to enroll directly in a four-year institution. Community colleges, with their long history of providing an education to a population that is often low-income, immigrant, and less academically prepared, are better positioned to help these students achieve success in their first postsecondary experiences. He noted that,

> Among students for whom English is not their first language, standardized testing is a very difficult way to indicate what their natural ability is. But within the context of the community college that performance can be shown and be proven, and through graduation and maintaining a high grade point average the opportunity to not only create access but to maintain academic integrity is preserved.

Templin concluded his remarks by noting one additional policy change that had affected public higher education in Virginia. The state legislature created a 'charter' status for the public universities, whereby, in return for more operational flexibility and autonomy, the institutions have agreed to help the Commonwealth achieve a number of educational goals, college access among them. So far, the College of William and Mary, the University of Virginia, and Virginia Tech have entered into these agreements. As part of these agreements, the three institutions have pledged to guarantee admission to students who are transferring from community colleges in the state and adhere to standard academic criteria. Thus, in combination with the Community College Transfer Scholarship, which will help to promote financial accessibility to the four-year institutions, students will also have a smoother path toward admissions accessibility.

After the TIAA-CREF conference concluded, the Virginia Legislature made a number of revisions to the program that Templin had outlined, most with the impact of reducing the generosity of the financial support. Legislation passed by both the House and Senate in March 2007 created the Two Year College Transfer Grant Program. Under this program, students transferring directly from any Virginia community college to a public or private four-year institution in the state would be eligible for an annual grant of $1000. To obtain the grant, the student must receive an associate degree from the community college with a grade point average (GPA) of at least 3.0, must maintain that GPA after he or she transfers, and must have demonstrated financial need (as evidenced by an expected family contribution of $8000 or less, which should bring the program up to the approximate income level Templin described in the earlier plan). Students who pursue a bachelor's degree program in engineering, mathematics, nursing, teaching or science will receive an additional $1000 annually in grant support.

## CONCLUSION

The speakers in this session presented a variety of perspectives on the relationship between institutional tuition pricing policies and student access. While federal and state governments play important roles in promoting access through their financial aid programs, institutional tuition and financial aid policies – in both the public and the private sectors of higher education – are playing an increasingly important role in helping to determine who gains access to the nation's colleges and universities.

The presentations summarized here represented four very different parts of the postsecondary system in the United States. James Garland described how a selective public university implemented an innovative policy that eliminated the distinction in tuition pricing between in-state and out-of-state students, and in doing so was able to increase the diversity of the institution. He used the changes at Miami University as a model for how an entire state public university system could be moved toward more of a market orientation in terms of state control and tuition pricing.

James Scannell, whose firm works with many less selective public and private institutions, presented a case study of how enrollment management analysis helped a tuition-dependent private college improve both efficiency and equity in its use of financial aid resources. The institution, a small Catholic college, was facing difficulty enrolling enough students to meet its target for the size of its freshman class. The college used Scannell's firm to help it examine its existing financial aid programs and come up with a better way to package aid so as to both meet enrollment goals and increase the socioeconomic diversity of its student body. While many observers have criticized the use of merit aid for enrollment management purposes, Scannell demonstrated how this institution used merit scholarships to effectively accomplish both equity and efficiency goals.

Catharine Hill, President of Vassar College, summarized a study she conducted with a colleague at Williams College that examined the distribution of students by income at a set of elite, private colleges and universities around the country. What they found, not surprisingly, was that students at these 28 institutions were very highly skewed toward the upper end of the income distribution, even though the institutions had relatively generous institutional need-based financial aid programs. To counter the argument that lower-income students were not able to gain admittance to these institutions owing to academic rather than financial barriers, they examined the pool of high-achieving students across the country. Finding that lower-income, high-achieving students were underrepresented at these institutions as compared with the pool nationwide, they concluded that other barriers must be getting in the way of their enrollment. They pointed to the possibility of financial barriers, as well as others, as the possible culprits.

Robert Templin, president of the nation's second largest community college in northern Virginia, discussed the growing demand for his institution and for higher education in general in that state. He described how Virginia has responded by implementing a new scholarship program that will allow graduates of community colleges to transfer to public four-year institutions and receive a state grant once they enroll there. The state is hoping this will encourage more students to begin their baccalaureate education at the community colleges – which are not just lower-priced institutions but also receive less subsidy through state appropriations – and thus maximize the use of public resources for supporting higher education.

The problem of increasing tuition prices, along with the changing nature of financial aid policies that was described at the beginning of this chapter, will likely continue to be on the public agenda into the future. Ensuring access, particularly for low-income students, will require a variety of policy responses on the part of governments and higher education institutions. This session at the TIAA-CREF Leadership Conference presented examples of how institutions and state governments can respond to these issues. These examples should be taken into consideration as the nation moves forward in addressing issues of affordability and access in higher education.

# NOTES

1. These figures were calculated by the author from the National Postsecondary Student Aid Study, a nationally representative survey of all college students conducted periodically for the US Department of Education (National Center for Education Statistics, 2004, 2005).
2. See Holtschneider (1997), for example, on the awarding of institutional financial aid during the early years of higher education in the United States.
3. See Davis (2003), Haycock (2006), Hubbell and Lapovsky (2002) and Redd (2000) for data and analyses of these trends.
4. The Williams College economics department has become a laboratory for the development of college presidents with a background in studying higher education. In addition to Hill, other former Williams economics faculty who went on to become presidents in recent years include Michael McPherson at Macalester College, Stephen Lewis at Carleton College, and Morton Owen Schapiro at Williams.
5. See Lewis and Winston (1997) for more on the relationship between the cost of education, prices paid by students, and the subsidies they receive.
6. See for example Bowen et al. (2005), Carnevale and Rose (2004), and Heller (2004) for recent analyses of this issue.
7. Hill and Winston did not have SAT data for individual students at the COFHE schools, so the distribution for all COFHE students is compared with the national

distribution at a variety of SAT levels indicative of the degree of selectivity at the COFHE schools. Therefore, the COFHE distribution remains the same for each SAT level comparison.
8. Again, the COFHE distribution does not control for SAT.
9. While this rate is low relative to Virginia's four-year public institutions, it is slightly higher than the national average for community colleges, which was $2272 in 2006–2007 (College Board, 2006a).

# REFERENCES

Bowen, W.G., M.A. Kurzweil and E.M. Tobin (2005), *Equity and Excellence in American Higher Education*, Charlottesville: University of Virginia Press.

Breneman, D.W. (1994), *Liberal Arts Colleges: Thriving, Surviving, or Endangered?*, Washington, DC: The Brookings Institution.

Breneman, D.W. (2003), 'Why a public college wants to send in-state tuition soaring', *The Chronicle of Higher Education*, 25 April, B20.

Carnevale, A.P. and S.J. Rose (2004), 'Socioeconomic status, race/ethnicity, and selective college admissions', in R.D. Kahlenberg (ed.), *America's Untapped Resource: Low-income Students in Higher Education*, Washington, DC: Century Foundation Press, pp. 101–56.

Colavecchio-Van Sickler, S. (2006), 'Too cheap to be great', *St. Petersburg Times*, 8 October, 1P.

College Board (2006a), *Trends in College Pricing, 2006*, Washington, DC: author.

College Board (2006b), *Trends in Student Aid, 2006*, Washington, DC: author.

Davis, J.S. (2003), *Unintended Consequences of Tuition Discounting*, Indianapolis, IN: New Agenda Series, Lumina Foundation for Education.

*Dayton Daily News* (2003), 'Miami's plan for tuition hike doesn't add up', 4 May, B6.

Haycock, K. (2006), *Promise Abandoned: How Policy Choices and Institutional Practices Restrict College Opportunities*, Washington, DC: The Education Trust.

Heller, D.E. (2004), 'Pell Grant recipients in selective colleges and universities', in R.D. Kahlenberg (ed.), *America's Untapped Resource: Low-income Students in Higher Education*, Washington, DC: Century Foundation Press, pp. 157–66.

Heller, D.E. (2006), *Merit Aid and College Access*, Madison: Wisconsin Center for the Advancement of Postsecondary Education, University of Wisconsin.

Higher Education Act of 1965, Pub. L. No. 89-329 (1965).

Hill, C.B. and G.C. Winston (2006a), 'Access: net prices, affordability, and equity at a highly selective college', *Economics of Education Review*, **25** (1), 29–41.

Hill, C.B. and G.C. Winston (2006b), 'How scarce are high-ability, low-income students?', in M.S. McPherson and M.O. Schapiro (eds), *College Access: Opportunity or Privilege?*, New York: The College Board.

Hill, C.B., G.C. Winston and S.A. Boyd (2005), 'Affordability: family incomes and net prices at highly selective private colleges and universities', *The Journal of Human Resources*, **40** (4), 769–90.

Holtschneider, D.H. (1997), 'Institutional aid to New England college students: 1740–1800', unpublished doctoral dissertation, Harvard University, Cambridge, MA.

Hubbell, L.L. and L. Lapovsky (2002), 'Tuition discounting: results from NACUBO's annual survey indicate increases in tuition discounting', *NACUBO Business Officer*, **35** (8), 24–33.

La Ganga, M.L. (2006), 'A money gap and a brain drain; UC Berkeley, long on reputation but short on funding, is losing talent', *Los Angeles Times*, A1.

Lewis, E.G. and G.C. Winston (1997), 'Subsidies, costs, tuition, and aid in US higher education: 1986–87 to 1993–94' (No. DP-41), Williamstown, MA: Williams Project on the Economics of Higher Education.

National Center for Education Statistics (2004), 'National Postsecondary Student Aid Study 1992–1993 data analysis system', retrieved 10 December from http://nces.ed. gov/dasol/

National Center for Education Statistics (2005), 'National Postsecondary Student Aid Study 2003–2004 data analysis system', retrieved 7 June from http://nces.ed.gov/dasol/

Redd, K.E. (2000), *Discounting toward Disaster: Tuition Discounting, College Finances, and Enrollments of Low-income Undergraduates*, Indianapolis, IN: USA Group Foundation.

Scannell & Kurz, Inc. (2007), Scannell & Kurz website, retrieved 7 February from http://www.scannellkurz.com/

Thomson, S.C. (2007), 'Is it a shell game?', *National Crosstalk*, **15** (Winter), 3–5.

US Census Bureau (2007a), 'Income – median family income in the past 12 months by family size', retrieved 5 February from http://www.census.gov/hhes/www/income/medincsizeandstate.html

US Census Bureau (2007b), 'Race and Hispanic origin of householder – households by median and mean income: 1967 to 2005' [on-line data file], retrieved 15 January from http://www.census.gov/hhes/www/income/histinc/h05.html

# 6. Perspectives on transformational change from the TIAA-CREF experience

**Herbert M. Allison Jr**

The theme of the TIAA-CREF Institute's 2006 conference, Transformational Change in Higher Education: Positioning Your Institution for Future Success, reflects the unprecedented set of challenges facing the great majority of America's universities and colleges. Over time, every institution is confronted with challenges which require it to change. For the past 25 or 30 years, corporate America has had to confront growing pressures for change – technology, globalization, transformation of the workforce, new regulations, and the growing 'power' of shareholders, to list a few. Some leading companies have coped well, but most have not, so there has been remarkable turnover in the composition of the Fortune 500. Even venerable companies are faltering as they try to manage in a new competitive environment.

For higher education, the decades to come may bring changes just as dramatic. Some of the forces for change are similar to those in industry – technology and globalization, for example. Other forces, some of which were discussed throughout the conference, are different: funding; the widening gap between investment returns of large and small endowments; the possibility for taxation of some schools' activities; and changes in laws on affirmative action. A wide variety of institutions were represented at the conference, each with a distinct mission and challenges. Each institution must chart its own course, so I am not going to presume to suggest solutions. What I *can* describe is the general challenge of leading change, based on what I have learned leading a transformation at TIAA-CREF. That process has taught me about the principles that can help leaders in organizations of any kind respond effectively to changes in environment and ensure the ongoing success of their institutions.

At TIAA-CREF, we have set about evolving to better meet the needs of our institutional clients and individual participants. I have had to think a lot about how a leader can cause an institution to embrace necessary change, and how that leader can institutionalize continual change so that the institution can stay in tune with its environment and prosper far into the future.

## HOW CAN AN INSTITUTION BE CAUSED TO EMBRACE THE NEED FOR CHANGE?

At TIAA-CREF, that was a major challenge. After all, we had been very successful for over 80 years. The company became great by inventing a remarkably effective, portable retirement plan. The plan was simple – just two investment products that were diversified and safe. Our customers did not have to manage their savings; our company did that. In some cases, participants retired on *more* annual income than they ever earned in working years. And a portion of their TIAA retirement income was guaranteed for life.[1]

In our certainty that *our* way was best for those we serve, we became blinded to the changing needs of our individual and institutional clients. Growing numbers of individuals desired not only more investment choices, but also tailored advice about which products to choose. We did not offer much choice *or* investment advice. And because our computer systems were originally built for just two investment products, they could not easily support more choices, or provide convenient record-keeping services that institutions needed. We were internally focused in the way we operated. We made decisions based on our own view of what was best for clients, rather than methodically seeking input from those clients.

In our core market – not-for-profit institutions – we devoted our main attention to those we already served. We ignored the growing trend of non-profit institutions and their newer employees toward selecting other vendors. We also dismissed the fact that we had not won any competitive bids for contracts with large institutions for many years.

For too long, TIAA-CREF defined its market in terms of its own business model. We rejected even considering broader definitions of our customers' needs – because changing to meet those broader needs would have been too disruptive. The pain and uncertainty of change, the risk of losing the presumed safety and comfort of our traditional practices, seemed greater than the possible benefits of adapting to changing preferences and new opportunities. Our competitors had already taken notice, however, and began aggressively seeking out our customers. We had to embrace change, no matter how painful, in order to compete and even survive.

In meetings and conversations with senior academic leaders across the country over the past four years, we have heard about a number of the challenges institutions are confronting, including those mentioned earlier. They are grappling with changing demographics of students, shifts in the composition of faculty and administrators, burgeoning applications and enrollments, and growing demands for access. There also is intensifying competition from traditional and non-traditional competitors such as foreign institutions and for-profit companies offering courses online and in local facilities.

All these changes and others are occurring amid growing pressures on costs and revenues. On the cost side, budgets are being squeezed by demand for new facilities, cutting-edge technology, and enhanced amenities for students and faculty. On the revenue side, rising prices for tuition, enabling equal access, and changing patterns of financial aid are becoming increasingly political issues, constraining institutions' ability to offset increases in costs.

Public universities are facing the long-term prospect of reductions in government funding. Studies show that all 50 states will face budget deficits by about 2013, driven mainly by the rapidly increasing costs of Medicaid, which could crowd out government spending for education and infrastructure.

For private universities, the already rich are getting richer. Those institutions are attracting the best investment managers and investment opportunities, and realizing much higher investment returns. Many institutions, even those whose endowments are among the largest, are launching unprecedented capital campaigns. In fact, according to published reports, 25 universities are currently attempting to boost their endowments by $1 billion or more. Several have announced campaigns to raise $3–5 billion each. The pressures on mid-size and small private institutions to keep pace will be acute.

And as much as it is desirable to educate the public about the importance of higher education and the vital role it plays in a knowledge economy, the fact is that funding of higher education, both public and private, will remain under pressure from competing priorities – entitlements for healthcare, K-12 education, infrastructure repair, and national defense, to name a few.

In addition, higher taxes in the future are likely to crimp donations from the affluent people who provide most gifts to endowments. The scarcity of resources, on one hand, and the need to continually upgrade education programs, facilities and access, on the other, will inevitably force difficult choices on all kinds of higher education institutions. If institutions are to be successful, those choices will involve making fundamental decisions about their priorities and will require previously unthinkable transformation in programs and infrastructure. At the same time, new opportunities are appearing which offer possibilities for institutions of higher education to serve their fundamental mission even more effectively while also controlling costs and pricing in the years ahead.

One of these opportunities is new technology to reduce the cost of access to information and of connecting faculty and students. This holds possibilities not only for distance learning but also for reducing costs on campus.

Another opportunity is increasing the numbers of partnerships between institutions to provide breadth of curriculum and access to excellence in teaching. It also will be increasingly feasible for institutions to gain efficiencies by breaking down their vertically integrated structures in which they provide everything from faculty to recreation to facilities for dining. Already, growing numbers of colleges and universities are making changes that were inconceivable even a decade ago. Some are sharing courses and faculty, outsourcing parts of their administrative support, building their brands through advertising, putting courses on the Web and forming partnerships with business to foster research, attract and retain talent and bolster the local economy. Others are substituting adjunct professors for tenure-track ones, encouraging ventures to market intellectual property and building or adopting high schools to expand the pipeline of qualified students. Ultimately, institutions will need a blank-sheet approach to redesigning their enterprise in ways that enable them not only to continually improve their core functions of teaching and research but also to expand their outreach to more students while reducing the cost of education to consumers of it.

At TIAA-CREF, we have had to make these kinds of difficult choices. Our pricing is constrained by our mission to be a provider of world-class financial and retirement services and by increasing competition from world-class institutions working hard to displace us from leadership in the not-for-profit sector. Even as we reinvent our entire market offering and introduce new technology and broader products and services, we have had to reduce our existing cost base by $300 million per year.

Needless to say, this has been disruptive and painful for all but it has opened up a new path to growth and to fulfilling our historic mission, all while reducing our expense ratio and thereby better enabling participants to keep more of the returns they earn through our investments. We have had to pare down to the essentials to meet client needs – there is no room for anything extraneous to that mission. For example, we have sold an entire city block of office towers in mid-town Manhattan, which formerly were entirely occupied by our employees. We wedged many employees into TIAA-CREF's New York headquarters, and relocated several thousand others to what is now our largest location in Charlotte, North Carolina, and to regional offices all over the country.

## SO HOW CAN A LEADER CAUSE AN INSTITUTION TO EMBRACE CHANGE?

I do not believe that any leader can compel an organization to make fundamental change by logical arguments or force of authority. That is certainly the case in higher education, where there are very powerful constituents: faculty, alumni, boards of trustees. The organization will resist passively or even actively for as long as it takes until the CEO or the president gives up, retires or is forced out.

The only way to bring about the kind of sweeping change essential to restoring leadership is to enable people to see for themselves that change is imperative. People need to feel that, for institutions, the penalties of resisting change are even greater than the costs of changing, and that the opportunities exceed the short-term costs.

When I arrived at TIAA-CREF in late 2002, I realized that I could not impose the required changes on an organization that was convinced it was doing well and knew only one way of doing things. Instead, I asked a number of middle managers – people with extensive experience, whose views would carry weight and who did not have to defend the status quo – to form teams to study our market position, our customers' needs, our technological capabilities, our

HR policies and programs, our financial situation and our investment performance, and then to recommend our strategy going forward. I reckoned that if they had the same facts as I did, they would want to do what I would do.

After six months of hard work, they recommended changes more radical than I could have hoped for or imposed myself. And because those people strongly advocated the changes to their colleagues throughout the organization, and then were promoted to positions where they could lead them, we have moved ahead rapidly with a total transformation of our business model. We are introducing many new products and services, adopting open architecture (other companies' products on our platform), expanding our office network around the country to personalize us with clients, and transferring our operations to new systems that are more flexible and responsive.

In the academic world, there are great examples of comprehensive change. For example, when John Pepper, formerly the Chairman and CEO of Procter & Gamble, stepped down from chairing the Yale Corporation in 2004 to become the University's vice president for finance and administration, he faced a $30 million budget deficit, strained labor relations and an enormous campus renovation project. He responded with a more transparent, inclusive process for achieving necessary cost reductions and redirecting funds toward Yale's core mission of teaching and research. As a result, he received support from the very people whose organizational units would have to change. Leaders need to be sensitive to the concerns of students and faculty, alumni, government officials, providers of research dollars and others. But leaders also need to ensure that their key constituents understand the forces compelling change. If they do, the need for comprehensive transformation, as contrasted with narrower, programmatic changes, will become clearer.

The key to helping an institution embrace change is to encourage stakeholders at many levels – students, staff, faculty, administrators, unions, policymakers – to gather the facts, grapple with them, agree on an operating model as if they were starting new today, and commit to whatever changes are required to implement that model. Only by encouraging people to deal with the issues themselves and recommend what *they* would do can leaders generate real buy-in, a sense of urgency, and ownership of systemic change.

That brings us to the next question.

# HOW CAN A LEADER INSTITUTIONALIZE CONTINUAL CHANGE SO THAT THE INSTITUTION CAN STAY IN TUNE WITH ITS ENVIRONMENT AND PROSPER FAR INTO THE FUTURE?

It takes relentless discipline to stay focused on meeting the fundamental, broadly defined needs of consumers of services – however that consumer is defined – rather than lapse into the more comfortable state of preserving an operating model or meeting short-term goals. At TIAA-CREF, adopting the discipline of consumer focus has meant transforming virtually all elements of our business – products, distribution, technology, compensation, pricing, financial and service metrics, marketing and organizational structure – all at once. Because all these elements of the enterprise are interdependent, changing one element usually leads to changing all the others, so that all elements will again be compatible and reinforce each other in an optimal way.

Few organizations are willing to undertake such daunting change unless they face an immediate crisis. That is why they deny the need to change longer than they should and defer the actual changes even longer. If they are going to continually realign their priorities, structures and operations with the changing realities of their environment, institutions must *define* their long-term mission *broadly* in a way that is lasting – for example, 'to meet the financial needs of customers on the best terms practicable' – as Andrew Carnegie did for TIAA. Then they must *design* the organization to be always alert for new, better methods for meeting that fundamental need and to embrace, rather than resist, continual transformation. For us, designing a client-focused, adaptive company requires placing much of the decision-power with managers and employees closest to the customers. It has also required that we tell ourselves the truth about changes in customers' needs, about best practices in the industry, and about the company's performance in meeting needs and achieving world-class standards. Above all, we must ensure that employees and other constituents – trustees, rating agencies, regulators and even our customers – have the unvarnished facts. Only when they are well informed can they come to appreciate and wholeheartedly support continual change, and bear the personal uncertainties that go with it.

Institutions of higher education must also be willing to renovate their operating models continually and profoundly, if necessary, while remaining true to their mission of teaching and research and their values of independent inquiry and academic integrity. As we have learned at TIAA-CREF, you have to be careful not to mistake traditions and habits for mission and values. It is important to distinguish the things that should never change – academic independence, tolerance for dissent, and so on – from the things that must constantly change, such as short-term priorities, budgets, technology and curricula. Even as we change every aspect of how we do business at TIAA-CREF, we are not changing our mission one iota. Our focus will remain the not-for-profit community; we will not pay employees commissions for selling products;[2] we will maintain our not-for-profit heritage and values; and that means we certainly will not go public. In fact, by changing to better meet our customers' needs, we are reconnecting with our timeless mission.

For institutions to sustain continued change so that they can survive and prosper into the future, they will need to shift their attention and scarce resources, as much as possible, from activities that are not central to their distinctive mission and identity to activities that are – teaching and research. To do that, institutions will have to employ their core values, their independent, objective, fact-based method of inquiry, to examine their own situations, and then make changes that the facts demand – even if those changes are broad, unsettling and difficult. Transformative change that restores harmony between an institution, its environment and the needs of its constituents is far less risky than clinging to comfortable but outmoded traditions.

As leaders, whether of companies, colleges or universities, we have the daunting responsibility of summoning our constituents to gather and contend with the facts themselves, and then encourage them to embrace the need for continuous change to meet our steady purpose, in order that our institutions can remain successful over the long run.

# NOTES

1. Any guarantees under annuities issued by TIAA are subject to TIAA's claims-paying ability.
2. Our advisors receive no commissions. They are compensated through a salary-plus-incentive program.

# Index